CHRIS ROBERTS

TOM JONES

TOM JONES

CHRIS ROBERTS

TED SMART

First published in 1999 by
Virgin Books
An imprint of
Virgin Publishing Limited
Thames Wharf Studios,
Rainville Road,
London W6 9HT

This edition produced for
The Book People Ltd
Hall Wood Avenue
Haydock
St Helens
WA11 9UL

A catalogue record for the book is
available from the British Library

ISBN 1 85227 846 3

Text pages designed by
Michael Bell Design

Colour Origination by Colourwise ltd

Printed and bound in Great Britain by Jarrold Books

PICTURE CREDITS

All Action
65
Julian Barton 87
D. Dadds 137
Doug Peters 108
Duncan Raban 157

Alpha
15, 25, 37, 53, 55, 76, 91, 97, 99, 110, 113, 150, 144, 156
Alec Byrne 140
Dave Bennett 101, 123, 130
R. Chambury 135
Paul Harris 59, 97, 127, 139
Dave Parker 153

Famous
Pat Little 114

Pictorial Press
2, 3, 6, 8, 10, 11, 17, 18, 19, 20, 21, 22, 26, 28, 31, 32, 33, 34, 38, 40, 43, 44, 48, 51, 56-57, 64, 67, 68-9, 71, 79, 84, 85, 93, 94, 104

Redferns
Richie Aaron 92
George Chin 115
Patrick Ford 77, 121, 151
Gems 41
Mick Hutson 133
Bob King 131
T. Manley 52
Michael Ochs Archives 47

Retna
Neal Preston 1, 100, 124, 143, 149, 154
Steve Pyke 159

Rex Features
14, 24, 72, 97, 103, 105, 107, 128
Dave Hogan 147
Nils Jorgensen 82
Sunday Magazine 134
Brian Rasic 118
Richard Young 148

Ronald Grant Archive
4, 73, 81, 88, 152, 155

Angela Lubrano
117

*'Every day when I wake up
I thank the Lord I'm Welsh.'*

INTRODUCTION

IT'S NOT
UNUSUAL

On BBC Wales, a commercial for the channel is screened frequently. It saves its biggest 'star' contribution for its finale. Therein, a beaming Tom Jones announces, 'Every day when I wake up I thank the Lord I'm Welsh.' This tells us at least three things about Tom. One, he's pleased to be *au fait* with the lyrics and catchphrases of contemporary bands (in this case, Cerys Matthews' Catatonia). Two, he's proud of his homeland. And three, it's proud of him: after well over 30 years as a showbiz legend, he's still its biggest household name.

Tiger Tom, The Twisting Vocalist. That's how Tom Jones, born the son of a coalminer in 1940, was illustriously billed in his early days playing working men's clubs in the Welsh valleys. As the sixties began, Jones, then still known by his real name of Tom Woodward, was struggling. Already a married father, neither he nor anybody else in that part of the country had a clue as to what was fashionable, hip or happening in the fast-moving world of pop. They hadn't seen many electric guitars. Woodward enjoyed nothing more than belting out rock 'n' roll standards in front of a drunken crowd of mates. He was confident wider appreciation would come – everybody told him so. He just didn't know how.

Then Gordon Mills, a smart songwriter, manager, and local-boy-made-good, went
to see him perform. Mills knew at once that this wild, wanton Welshman, with the voice
of a soul man and the hips of a gyroscope, could be a global superstar. He wasn't the next
Beatles; Mills realised that. His appeal was too physical, in many ways already a throwback
to the pelvis-propelled rockers of the fifties. There was nothing androgynous whatsoever
about him. He was unapologetically masculine. He'd woo the grown-ups, the women who'd
given up bobby-soxing. And with that titanic, sensational voice, he'd do it if it meant
breaking down brick walls.

Things didn't fall into place immediately for Tom, vocalist of Tommy Scott And
The Senators, once he hit London. Starving in a Ladbroke Grove hovel with the boys from
his band, now called The Squires, he despaired, even considering suicide. He made a
record. It flopped. Tom thought about giving up and returning to South Wales. Although
he was hardly, if ever, short of female company, he missed his wife and son.

He was seen as a serious rival and heir to Elvis Presley, who he befriended.

A song came along, co-written by Gordon, but he'd promised it to Sandie Shaw as
her follow-up to 'Always Something There To Remind Me'. Tom and the boys were furious.
Oddly, Sandie Shaw turned the song down, so Tom gladly recorded it. Released in January
1965, 'It's Not Unusual' went to number one in the singles chart on 1 March, St David's
Day. Tom, on tour with Cilla Black and Tommy Roe at the time, celebrated by drinking
till dawn. This was something he'd always done. And always would.

The press found out that, contrary to his publicity, he was married: pop stars with
'sexy' images rarely owned up to wedded bliss at the time. There have been numerous
occasions since when Tom has been economical with the truth, and many of these have
occurred in the proximity of glamorous female pop stars, former Miss Worlds, and suchlike.
Wife Linda is the very definition of long-suffering. And has never, since the early days,
been strapped for cash. There have been public and private spats, but she's still there,
in Wales. Often while Tom and most of the family are living in California.

After 'It's Not Unusual' sped into the American Top Ten, the hits kept on coming
through the late sixties and early seventies. Though Tom Jones isn't in the premier league

Tom performing with
The Moody Blues on a 1960s
TV show.

He's a handsome devil who says that 'looking back, the struggles were worth it.'

He's owned more Rolls-Royces than he's faced paternity suits.

all-time record sellers (he's had twelve UK Top Ten albums, but most of his vast fortune has been made through consistently sold-out live performances), it's remarkable how many of his heyday hits are to this day recognisable, and profoundly lovable, within seconds of their kicking in. There have been film theme songs: 'What's New Pussycat?' and 'Thunderball'. There have been big, blue ballads like 'Green, Green Grass Of Home', 'Delilah', 'Till', 'I'm Coming Home' and '(It Looks Like) I'll Never Fall In Love Again'. And there have been the ones sung, undoubtedly, by Tiger Tom The Twisting Vocalist – 'Help Yourself', 'She's A Lady', 'Detroit City'. More recently, there have been comeback hits – 'The Boy From Nowhere', 'Kiss'. There may well be still more just around the corner – Tom's been working on an album of duets with some of today's brightest, most boisterous young stars, from Catatonia to Robbie Williams, Manic Street Preachers to Stereophonics, all of whom, Welsh or otherwise, adore him. To be titled *Reload!*, it surfaces in September 1999.

Tom, after establishing his own hugely successful weekly television show in Britain (the entertainment world's biggest names queued up to appear on it), took off to America, where his show took top ratings on ABC. He was seen as a serious rival and heir to Elvis Presley, who he befriended. Many pairs of knickers were thrown at Tom's twinkling feet. This ritual survives, despite his reservations. He was courted by the era's most stellar showbiz celebrities. He never cracked Hollywood, though for a time such a move was planned, but he conquered Vegas. Some say his legendary, sweaty, euphoric live concerts single-handedly made it what it's become today – for better or worse. When Tom ruled the town, its morale entered a new golden age. In 1974, Tom toasted his birthday backstage with, among others, Debbie Reynolds and Liberace. Muhammad Ali once 'accidentally' punched him in the mouth. It wasn't the only time his face was rearranged: Tom has repeatedly and unabashedly undergone plastic surgery, shrugging that otherwise he'd only blow the money on yet another diamond ring.

But as Tom became a fixture of the American lounge circuit, he became a stranger to the British charts. He signed a near-disastrous, long-term deal to make country albums in Nashville. The formula Gordon had devised for his earlier period had dried up. Then Gordon died, of cancer. Pushing 50, in the late eighties, it seemed that Tom Jones's days as a marquee name were up.

A new manager came to the rescue. He advised Tom to jettison the country schlock, rediscover his rock 'n' roll roots and get in touch with some of the newer, funkier music being made. In '88, his cover of Prince's 'Kiss', with The Art Of Noise, put him back in the Top Ten. He moved on to working with more left-field, non-mainstream acts, even naming an album *The Lead and How To Swing It*. He matched Robbie Williams for cocky swagger at the Brit Awards in '98. Space and Catatonia enjoyed a hit singing his praises in 'The Ballad Of Tom Jones'. The new manager also recommended Tom play up his sense of irony; take a look at his sex-god, supersoft-porn image and fool around, have a little fun with it. Send up the hunky macho dawg thing; let a new generation know he was in on the joke. It paid dividends: he's been perceived differently, and with more affection, ever since. He even guested on *The Simpsons*. The new manager was doing a fine job. The new manager was Tom and Linda's previously shy, gauche son, Mark.

Tom may have been accused of chauvinism in his time, but he's always pretty much agreed with his accusers. He is, by now, a beloved national institution: the granddad from Treforest near Pontypridd who became a multi-millionaire international heartthrob. Barely a month goes by without some 'scandal' rocking the Sunday tabloids: another 'buxom blonde' having been 'seduced' by the demon 'love rat'. It all fuels the myth. It all helps the incredible longevity.

He is a rogue and a prince.
He is a bit of a chap, and then some.

He's been described as 'sweat personified' and – he hates this one – 'the man who made the Chippendales possible'. He's been called the Welsh Sinatra. As a teenager he was shoved through the glass door of a chip shop, but immediately chased after his assailant. Wilson Pickett told him he was 'the only white man who can sing soul'. He's owned more Rolls-Royces than he's faced paternity suits. He has homes in Bel Air, California and South Wales, having now sold Dean Martin's old house to Nicolas Cage. He's always enjoyed the trappings and glitz of stardom to the full. He's a handsome devil who says that 'looking back, the struggles were worth it.' Once incarcerated in Caracas for alleged violence, Tom has always taken a firm anti-drugs stance. He is a rogue and a prince. He is a bit of a chap, and then some. He'll tour Britain and America, revisiting *Reload!*, throughout the second half of 1999. In June 2000 he'll celebrate his 60th birthday. With, one imagines, considerable gusto.

His is a rags-to-riches story of textbook implausibility, blind youthful faith and shrewdly sold mature talent.

He is Jones The Voice, Jones The Sex. There's a tiger in his tank. He's for real, and his story is distinctly unusual.

It was love at first sight.

CHAPTER ONE

TWO HALFPENNIES TO RUB TOGETHER

It was love at first sight, Tom Jones has always asserted. Melinda Trenchard lived just around the corner in Treforest in the Rhondda Valley. When they were little, Tom went to a Protestant junior school while she went to a Catholic one, so he didn't see as much of her as he would have liked until secondary modern. At the age of ten or eleven, he remembers walking down her street and finding her playing marbles. They shared their first kiss, and from that point on Tom reacted to his little friend in a new way.

So much so that the pair were married, and indeed parents, at sixteen. They tied the knot at Pontypridd Registry Office on 2 March 1957, and son Mark – whose destiny was to intertwine closely with his father's durable career – was born on 11 April. Young marriages weren't so out of the ordinary in Tom's milieu. Many of his friends had started working down the mines at fifteen, and as Tom put it, 'Once you're working you think you're a man.

As he entered his teens he became something of a tearaway, frequently missing school altogether, hanging out at the swimming baths and, some say, breaking into a tobacconists and stealing cigarettes.

In those awkward mid-teen years, Tom supposed that – realistically – he'd end up following his father down the mines. Career-wise, there didn't seem to be many options. And soon after he'd begun courting Linda (as Melinda was generally known), a surprising blow struck the strapping young lad. He went down with tuberculosis, in that era still a major, often fatal, illness, especially in poor, working-class districts. He was confined to bed for the best part of a year, his worried parents and various cousins nursing him as well as they could. It's been alleged by one hostile member of his extended family that he took the opportunity to make a pass at one cousin as she helped to look after him.

Laid up in bed, however, he couldn't attempt too much more than listening to music – always a pleasure – and drawing. He also, reportedly, ate well, becoming taller, stronger, even chubby, his brown hair blackening. 'When we met up again after he came back to school,' Linda once told a magazine, 'I didn't recognise him at first. But I was immediately attracted to him again!'

Soon Tom was out and about again, looking for trouble. And while he was defensively proud of his relationship with Linda, he also enjoyed time spent drinking in pubs with his mates and getting into fights, both of which he did from the age of thirteen or so. He was a big lad with a reputation and a healthy thirst. Most neighbours thought he fancied himself rotten, and there was a fair queue of local louts eager to bring him down to size. He didn't always win these petty scraps, hence the many-times-broken nose.

South Wales was and remains a 'hard' area, but in those days knives and weapons were for cowards – fists and head-butting were fair. One night, Tom was head-butted through the glass door of the chip shop. There had been, a few nights earlier, 'words'. The funny thing, Tom thought, was that it wasn't over a girl.

He was as much a lover as a fighter, however. To a Protestant kid, there was something attractively enigmatic about the local Catholic girls. For a start, they wore earrings. Tom and Linda began playing kiss-chase, and by age twelve had become all but inseparable. By the time Tom was fifteen and Linda fourteen, they'd become proper, grown-up, actual real-life 'lovers'. The great event occurred up a mountain, in the summertime. Tom has admitted that he was already fairly sexually experienced beforehand, so wasn't particularly obsessed about losing his virginity.

Chivalry wasn't dead in the fifties in Wales, however. Tom has spoken of his pride
in not bragging about his sweetheart, when asked by his mates if he'd 'given her one' yet.
Perhaps, to this day, female fans who've thrown their underwear at Tom fantasise safe in
the knowledge that he won't read out the nametag.

But true love arrived carrying lessons and responsibilities. Linda was still just fifteen
when she found out she was pregnant. Tom was sixteen. Although the Welsh mining
communities of the time were familiar with teenage pregnancies, this still signalled trauma
for the two youths, and their parents, who in grave, concerned voices tensely discussed
the situation.

Certainly, this was a crisis. An abortion was unthinkable, but on the other hand
the teenagers were surely too young to bring up a child. Maybe the child could be adopted.
Maybe Linda's waitress mum Vi could bring the baby up as her own. Linda sobbed loudly.
Tom sat silently, until his father said something he's always been grateful to him for.
Why, asked Tom Senior, are we talking about these two as if they're not in the room?
It's their life; let's hear from them. He looked at Tom and asked him what he wanted to do.
Tom said he wanted to marry Linda and she wanted to marry him.

Tom's mother and sister

Sheila, at home in Pontypridd.

Tom's father looked at him and said, "Go ahead."

As it turned out, the couple still had to wait until Linda was legally 'of age' (i.e. sixteen), in January '57. That March, they married, and moved into the basement of Linda's parents' house. With the birth of Mark, Tom, just out of school, now realised he had a family to support. He was excited, but the family didn't have two halfpennies to rub together. He worked nightshifts at a paper mill, and all the overtime he could, but couldn't afford to take the night off when Linda went into hospital.

His first job had been in a glove-making factory, as an apprentice. He was paid £2 a week, and hated every second. He'd moved on to the paper mill by the time of the wedding, but received a pittance there because he was so young. Times were hard, with three mouths to feed. After a year he took the situation by the scruff of the neck, marching up to the mill manager and demanding a man's wage for a man's work.

> ## His first job had been in a glove-making factory, as an apprentice. He was paid £2 a week, and hated every second.

After this the money was fine, relatively. The only trouble was that Tom knew he wanted to be a professional singer. What with nightshifts, the job was obviously in the way.

At 21, he quit the job, knowing he was now old enough to get the adult rate wherever he worked. The first few years of married life had been tough for Tom and Linda, but the aforementioned close relatives had been supportive. Tom was singing more and more at pubs, clubs, parties and concerts.

Tom began to make steady cash from his singing. His father had always dressed sharply, polishing the soles of his shoes and sporting an immaculately trimmed narrow moustache, and Tom emulated him, albeit with a slightly clearer eye for contemporary trends.

Soon, Tom was getting a local reputation as a smartly dressed layabout. His first tantalising glimpse of stardom wasn't far away.

Looking back, Tom shrugs off his unusually youthful marriage. 'We were sixteen and married with a baby, but we were happy,' he's said. 'We loved each other and had loving families nearby. In the valleys, you grow up quick. I didn't feel all that young.'

In 1989, many years and extra-curricular sexual shenanigans later, he told interviewer Emma Freud on British TV that, 'Marriage keeps me single; keeps me from marrying again! If I'd entered show business as a single man I'd probably have got married six or seven times by now, but my being already married meant I couldn't. Linda knows I couldn't do without the adulation from women, so she goes along with it.'

How happily Linda 'goes along' with this is a moot point: Tom's subsequent ascension to lasting fame as an only semi-parodic sex symbol, with regular alleged affairs, was to wipe the floor with any teenage indiscretions. The accompanying multi-millionaire status surely sweetened the pill.

Back in 1957, young Woodward discovered he was the father of a boy by ringing the hospital from a red telephone box which stood on Laura Street. Later, that very same phone box, bought and imported, stood proudly in the expansive grounds of tax exile Tom's Bel Air mansion, admired by such visitors as Michael Jackson.

He saw his chance and he gave it his best shot.

On the dole by day,
wild man of rock 'n' roll by night.

CHAPTER TWO

YOU SHOULD SEE THE OTHER BLOKE

On the dole by day, wild man of rock 'n' roll by night, Tom Woodward was soon giving it his all onstage most Friday evenings at the Pontypridd YMCA. When he became frontman for going-nowhere-fast local band The Senators, bassist and group leader Vernon Hopkins popped out to a phone box and picked up the directory. Something with an S, he thought to himself. He returned to his father's front room, where a crucial band meeting had just ended. 'Tommy Scott And The Senators,' he announced, to general approval. And so Tom Woodward became Tommy Scott, for a while.

Tom replaced their former vocalist Tommy Redman – real name Tommy Pittman – who'd found fronting the band to be a marginally less exciting activity than playing cards. After three consecutive Fridays of bumbling through without a singer, The Senators couldn't be blamed for sacking this Tommy. He was more into ballads, by his own

to wearing all-black leather. He soon became well known around the area. What with his dole money and his share of The Senators' takings, Tom had enough cash to indulge in his other favoured pastime. Twelve pints of bitter was considered an acceptable amount for Tom to have knocked back before ripping it up. Often the band would warm up the crowd with a few instrumentals while Tom warmed a barstool. If the singer spotted a young lady he fancied in the bar, the band might be left to play for longer than anticipated – on one occasion, 90 minutes. Yet Tom would always make his grand entrance at some point, so the band didn't complain. Besides, Tom was still rated as a major local hard-knock.

At a Caerphilly bar named the Green Fly, however, he was badly beaten up. 'Mind you,' he said quickly whenever anyone remarked on his cuts and bruises, 'you should see the other bloke.'

Though Tom's sweaty stage presence and cocky charisma were undeniable, the blossoming market was for fashionably fringed mods.

As the combo and their ultra-modern electric guitars nurtured a growing local reputation, this being the early sixties, pop music in Britain was undergoing a massive sea-change. Beatlemania and the Merseybeat boom had spun the music business on its head. Unknowns were rising swiftly through the non-existent ranks to instant national – and soon, international – celebrity.

Where would Tom and his Senators fit into the equation? Well, to be blunt, they wouldn't. Though Tom's sweaty stage presence and cocky charisma were undeniable, the blossoming market was for fashionably fringed mods. Tom's old-school rockers had the 'wrong' (Brylcreemed-back) hair and an unhip attitude. They weren't writing their own songs, and they certainly couldn't drop any arty or druggy references into the mix. They didn't 'get' mod, with its suits and speed. They'd fallen in love with the sounds of Chuck Berry, and Tom's perennial faves Jerry Lee Lewis and Little Richard. Fifties music, basically. Sure, The Beatles had started like that, but they were now taking massive strides forward. At home, people would shake their heads and mutter to Tom that he should get

At home, people would shake their heads and mutter to Tom that he should get over to London and show the English what it was all about.

over to London and show the English what it was all about, but when push came to shove, Tommy Scott And The Senators weren't at this stage sufficiently, or appropriately, 'cute'.

They had one only-temporarily-secret weapon, though – Tom. And before too long, the tiger's roar began to make waves. He'd done spots for BBC Wales on *Donald Peers Presents*, singing 'That Lucky Old Sun' – by his own admission 'bland' material, but it was a foot in the door. Local papers were beginning to pick up on the band. Then they were invited to support current number one act Billy J. Kramer And The Dakotas in Porthcawl. Tom, still largely unknown, drove the crowd into a frenzy. Kramer found it a tough act to follow. So tough, in fact, that after he'd finished just two numbers, the crowd hollered for more of Tom. Kramer was forced to cut his set short and allow The Senators a second set just to keep the peace. Not that there was much of what you'd call peace as Tom, now a master of the pelvis-thrusting sexual suggestion technique, raised the roof for a second time. His reputation grew.

Soon after this, following a Cardiff show by Jerry Lee Lewis, Tom chased Lewis's limo in a taxi until he procured his idol's autograph. It was to be one of the last times he played the role of fan rather than that of star.

He was realistic enough to take singing lessons, to assist his on-stage breathing. Friends and family remained supportive. Yet the very differentness that made him stand out was in some ways a hindrance – in Wales, the radio and television companies were markedly conservative, and booking agents and managers were thin on the ground, through lack of demand or necessity. Tom's since recalled that London, even then the Mecca of pop, seemed a very long way away (remember, at the time there were few fast trains or motorways). Tom didn't know a soul in London, anyway. 'So what was I going to do?' he's since said, shrugging. 'Walk around the streets singing to myself?'

He had his homeland in the palm of his hand, but how could he make contact with the outside world, where the scene – for all he could see on television or hear on radio – was all happening? Eventually he met two young songwriters, living in Wales, who promised to be the answer to his prayers. They weren't, as it turned out. In fact, the relationship ended in bitterness and acrimony, but at least it pointed Tom and his talents in the right direction.

Before too long, the tiger's roar began to make waves.

Raymond Godfrey and John Glastonbury wanted to make the big time every bit as much as Tom did. They would regularly travel to London-based publishers to tout their songs, until they were advised to find a group and get them to record the songs as a demo. And so their scouting expeditions began. The very next night they checked out three groups playing in Caerphilly, one of which knocked them sideways – Tommy Scott And The Senators. They introduced themselves, explained their plan, and found the band to be so clueless about business that they became their managers. This wasn't the easiest of jobs: they organised rehearsal time, but the group were often late or didn't turn up at all. However, they persisted, getting the group gigs, and eventually a tape was recorded, by some accounts in a Cardiff studio, by others in the toilets of the Pontypridd YMCA.

Godfrey and Glastonbury – or Myron and Byron, as the band took to sarcastically calling them – hawked the tape around London, to no avail. Just as all seemed futile, they visited one Joe Meek. A celebrated maverick, revered for his production on The Telstars' 1962 number one 'Telstar', Meek was an infuriating character who was notoriously difficult to work with. Years later, not many disagreed with *Record Mirror*'s obituary: 'Meek was a bullying, hot tempered and unpredictable character prone to constant mood swings. Not afraid of violence, he eventually turned it on himself and committed suicide.'

Desperate, and aware that Meek had contacts, the band recorded some songs with him. The release of a single was promised, a song called 'Lonely Joe' as an A-side, coupled with a Godfrey/Glastonbury composition, 'I Was A Fool'. For nine months Meek came up with excuses for the delay of its release. When he stopped taking their phone calls, the management pair banged on his front door and demanded an explanation. Tempers snapped all round, and the contract was torn up. Unfortunately, Meek kept the tapes.

'He taught me just about everything. He groomed me, taught me pacing. He said he'd guide me to be larger than life.'

Tom on Gordon Mills

So the long haul began again. Tom and the team returned to London and made another demo. In time Tom and the band became exasperated with Godfrey and Glastonbury's lack of success in giving them their big break. They were to agree to pass up managing him, in exchange for five per cent of his earnings, when another Welshman with London connections entered the picture. Born in the village of Tonypandy, he'd packed in working as a bus conductor and bravely forged a name for himself in the capital's music business, starting out as a harmonica player. This man was to prove the biggest single catalyst in transforming miner's boy Thomas Woodward into international crooner and gusset-soaker Tom Jones. His name was Gordon Mills.

He joined The Viscounts, who had two or three minor hits (one being a cover of the American smash, 'Who Put The Bomp?') as lead singer. But Gordon could write songs too, and soon was regularly delivering hits to Decca for acts such as Cliff Richard and Johnny Kidd And The Pirates, whose 'I'll Never Get Over You' he penned. Marrying a model, Jo, who was expecting their first daughter, he decided to concentrate on writing, and quit The Viscounts.

To Tommy Scott, twiddling his thumbs with frustration in Pontypridd and Treforest, Gordon seemed a mysterious, glamorous figure. To go from the Valleys to London – and make it! Mutual friends from musical Welsh families engineered their first meeting.

Tom toasting his success with Gordon Mills.

Many claim the credit to this day, among them Mills's school friend Gordon Jones, and local club singer Johnny Bennett. Mills was keen to dream up a ticket to big music-business money, and Tom was equally eager to be that ticket.

Bennett says he introduced the two men at a club in Porth one Sunday lunchtime. Gordon, home to visit his family, wasn't impressed by Tom's parochial scruffiness, although Bennett stressed that Tom was more fashion-conscious on stage. (Indeed, Tom would adopt a horses-for-courses strategy, donning black leather for younger audiences, and suits, or even a tuxedo and bow-tie, for older ones.) It seemed to Mills that everybody he spoke to was urging him to catch The Senators' show at the Top Hat in Cwmtellery that very evening. So he and wife Jo went along. The venue was so packed that Mills, big-shot from London or not, had to stand near a back door by the bar and crane his neck to see.

As soon as Tom took the stage, Mills knew he had what it takes. The opening bars, he's said, convinced him that Tom's voice could become the best on the face of the planet. The canny Senators, showing uncharacteristic if creepy business acumen, had opened the set with Mills's own 'I'll Never Get Over You', before Tom whirled into a scorching, soulful version of 'Spanish Harlem'.

All Tom needed, he reckoned, was to relocate to London where, he vowed, he'd find him a hit. Tom accepted this readily. He'd always known somebody would discover him, hadn't he? Thus began one of the most lucrative partnerships in showbiz history. An arrangement of sorts – later to veer into near-chaotic legal wranglings – was arrived at with Godfrey and Glastonbury, and Mills took the reins of Tom's career.

From this point onward, Tom took on board every suggestion Mills made. Stardom was inevitable – but not before a lean period of teething troubles in London. And not before another name change. One Tommy Scott was already active in the city, so Mills rechristened our man Tom Jones, cashing in on both his Welshness and the sexy hit movie, directed by Tony Richardson, of the time (1963). The Senators too needed a more hip, groovy, cosmopolitan moniker, so Mills came up with The Playboys. Tom Jones And The Playboys, in reality not all that sophisticated, were soon established in a fairly seedy two-room Ladbroke Grove flat, completely and utterly skint, Tom having left his patient wife and baby son back in South Wales. The adventure had begun.

*'It wasn't very hip to be Welsh
in those days.'*

CHAPTER THREE

'HE'S 22,
HE'S SINGLE, AND
HE'S A MINER!'

Bright lights, big city? Fame and fortune? Streets paved with gold? The naive Valley boys who constituted hopeful pop group Tom Jones And The Playboys were granted £1 a day each to live on. This placed them under great pressure when it came to making vital daily decisions, such as food or beer? Tough call...

Gordon Mills had made around £3,000 through the royalties on Johnny Kidd And The Pirates' 'I'll Never Get Over You'. His wife's earnings as a model were dropping since the birth of daughter Tracey. The Playboys' gigs paid between £30 and £50, then a decent sum, but after an early gig supporting The Rolling Stones at the 100 Club in Oxford Street, which they thought 'went well', there weren't enough bookings to make a living. Now and again they'd make a demo, but generally the lads didn't have much to do in London, and no money with which to do it. Gordon and Jo's overdraft grew.

Back in Wales, Tom's wife Linda went to work in the glove factory to feed herself and son Mark. Tom started to despair.

Yet the band remember there were good times amid these early struggles in London. Apart from original guitarist Mike Roberts, who'd elected to stick with his steady job as a cameraman, the lads were all in the same boat. Mickey Gee, who'd replaced Roberts, had quit his job with a Cardiff brewery to join the adventure. He was 21. Vernon Hopkins, the bassist who had initially recruited Tom, had left his niche as a printer for the *Pontypridd Observer*. He was 24, as was Tom. Rhythm guitarist Dave Cooper, whose parents ran an Abercynon hotel where the group had rehearsed, was 21, while drummer Chris Slade was just 17, a school-leaver. Every Saturday night the gang would get dressed up as best they could and head towards nearby Hammersmith in search of fun and frolics and post-teenage kicks.

The band had been better off financially in Wales. Friends would send hampers and sandwiches up to supplement the boys' meagre diet. But a 'one for all, all for one' spirit kept them going. They stayed up all night, drinking tea and waiting for things to happen. Fresh from the Valleys, dressed in Marks and Spencers shirts and with their hair slicked back, the Playboys weren't exactly the 'in' thing. As guitarist Mickey Gee has recalled, 'It wasn't very hip to be Welsh in those days.'

'I honestly thought that I'd had my big chance and failed. I was pretty miserable in those days.'

And, at 24, Tom was not the youngest of wannabe pop idols in a harsh business. He's confessed that at many auditions he was told his approach was 'too old-fashioned', 'too adult' or 'too fifties rock 'n' roll' for the kids. It was an era bursting with cute-faced, almost effeminate boy stars, from The Beatles to the Stones to Herman's Hermits. Next to these, he was perceived as a lorry driver, a bricklayer.

The novelty of being young men free in the big city began to wear off after about six months. And as another group called The Playboys were making a name for themselves, the group had to be rechristened yet again. This time they became The Squires.

Their front man couldn't understand why the breaks weren't forthcoming; why he was surviving on food parcels sent from home. He was the only member with a wife and son to support, and he wasn't doing that, as Linda may have been reminding him. Vernon came across him alone in the flat one day, crying and contemplating suicide. He pondered throwing himself under a Tube train at Notting Hill station, Vernon's since stated. A 'we're all in this together, we've stuck it out so far' pep talk from the bass player helped, but Tom still seemed set on giving up the dreams of glamour and returning to Wales. He'd even asked Gordon if he could send Linda £5, but Gordon admitted he'd already spent practically everything he had on keeping the band in town, and with Jo pregnant again and therefore not working, he was living on bank loans. Tom later commented that this was the worst six months of his life.

'Linda's always been wonderful when times were rough.'

Hope, however, springs eternal. In August 1964 Tom and the band released their first single, 'Chills And Fever', on Decca Records. Written by the team of Thompson and Gray, this was a thumping, buoyant belter with an untamed, ferocious vocal from Tom, but many critics considered it 'over-produced'. Listen closely and you can hear the kitchen sink. 'Chills And Fever', as in 'you're giving me...', was big in Pontypridd – chiefly because it was the first record anyone from the town had been involved with. Elsewhere, it sank without trace. (Today, it sounds great.) Years later, Tom told an interviewer, 'I honestly thought that I'd had my big chance and failed. I was pretty miserable in those days. You work hard for a recording break, then when you get it you think you're on your way. But it's only the beginning of the battles.'

He added, 'Linda's always been wonderful when times were rough. She always believed in me as a singer and gave me encouragement to go on trying. She knew that singing was what I wanted to do in life. You have to gamble if you want to get somewhere in this business.'

And having toughed out the drought, Tom was about to become the archetypal overnight sensation. Gordon Mills came good just when his disciples were beginning to entertain nagging doubts about his tactics. Even then, the Welshmen had to twist his arm, and at last enjoyed a slice of luck.

Tom and Linda at home
in Pontypridd.

Mills and sometime songwriting partner Les Reed (who was later involved with 'Delilah', 'I'm Coming Home' and 'Daughter Of Darkness') had come up with 'It's Not Unusual'. Trouble was, it had been commissioned by the management team of Sandie Shaw, who'd just had a smash hit with 'Always Something There To Remind Me'. Gordon badly wanted the follow-up assignment – Sandie was 'hot'. Gordon needed to make a demo of the song first, however, so The Squires were booked into a Denmark Street studio.

The track was laid down in twenty minutes. Mickey Gee played lead and rhythm guitar, and Chris Slade played tambourine, but Vernon Hopkins and Dave Cooper were flummoxed by its odd bossa nova rhythms. The group unanimously felt this was the song to give them a guaranteed hit. Gordon felt he had to keep his word to Sandie Shaw's people, but conceded that if they turned the song down, it was Tom's.

Bizarrely, Sandie Shaw *did* turn down 'It's Not Unusual'. Surely now it'd be plain sailing for Tom and The Squires? Not quite. Mills was losing faith in the boys' ability and thought Tom's voice required pro session men. So much for 'all for one'. From now on, The Squires were to be Tom's backing band, hired hands.

Alan Freeman declared 'It's Not Unusual' to be 'a pop landmark.'

The Ivy League were brought in as back-up singers and the new sessions took place at Decca's West Hampstead studios. Still, the right permutation of sounds couldn't be agreed on. Eventually, after many abortive takes, Peter Sullivan threw in the now-legendary brass section parts. Tom, quite sensibly, wondered if this would go down well at a time when guitars were fashionable and omnipotent, but agreed that the results were terrific.

The frustrations weren't over yet. Decca kept postponing the release date of 'It's Not Unusual', and with money at an all-time low, Gordon Mills had to advise the band to go home to Wales for Christmas because he couldn't afford to offer them even the merriment of their daily pound. Secretly, he and wife Jo, who sadly lost their unborn baby at this time, feared the lads wouldn't come back. Tom returned to the basement of his mother-in-law's house at 3 Cliff Terrace.

On St David's Day
the new Welsh singing sensation stood
astride the national charts.

Tom travelled back to London full of optimism, and the record was finally released in late January, 1965. BBC Radio didn't take to it, considering it 'too hot'. The offshore Radio Caroline loved it, and the then Radio Luxembourg DJ Alan Freeman playlisted it at once. With hindsight, he later declared 'It's Not Unusual' to be 'a pop landmark.' With Tom performing out of his skin on such TV shows as *Ready, Steady, Go!*, *Top Gear* and *Scottish Round-Up*,

the single entered the charts at number 21. Live bookings around the country accelerated (with Tom climbing the bill), and by early February the song was at number fifteen (and already number one in Pontypridd). Soon Tom was the first Welsh pop singer since Maureen Evans to make the Top Ten. By 22 February it was number two, and on 1 March, St David's Day, the new Welsh singing sensation stood astride the national charts, hollering, 'Why can't this crazy love be mine?'

Tom celebrated long and hard. He'd also benefited, in the early part of '65, from comparisons with P. J. Proby, an American singer exiled in the UK whose hips showed similar Elvis Presley influences, but whose wits (and popularity) deserted him when he 'accidentally' split his trousers onstage once too often. Meanwhile, Gordon was telling Tom exactly where to draw the line: he was to go far, loins-wise, but not too far. When Proby was kicked off Cilla Black's national tour, Tomwas quickly engaged as a replacement. Tom had to convert die-hard Proby fans carrying 'We want P. J.' banners, and did so.

Gordon's first press releases had boldly stated of Tom, 'He's 22, he's single, and he's a miner!' What the girl fans might have wanted, yes, but also in every way untrue. It didn't take long for the newspapers to cotton on and 'expose' the latest number one pop star. Hip-Swivelling Man Married With A Son Shock Horror!! Tom was embarrassed, and admitted that he didn't feel it was fair on Linda and Mark.

Some have said that the experiences of this hectic period have coloured the way Linda perceives the music industry, and Tom's career, ever since (it was Tom and Linda's eighth wedding anniversary the week 'It's Not Unusual' topped the charts). She's never been a 'showbiz person', and is naturally friendly but shy. This, though, was the sixties, and saucy sexual imagery and innuendo were essential to the selling of Tom Jones. Undergarments would soon be hurled.

The Squires, even though they weren't actually on the record, were delighted to join in any associated festivities. No more surviving on £1 a day! In Pontypridd, Tom's dad was surrounded by workmates when he emerged from the mines after a shift. They thrust the newspapers in front of his face – 'Look, your Tom's got to number one!' – followed by champagne and whisky down at the local club. Tom Junior lapped it all up, figuring success had arrived none too soon.

'Listen, Tommy boy, you might be a big shot up in London, but down in Pontypridd you wipe your shoes when you come in.'

C H A P T E R   F O U R

THUNDERBALL

'Listen, Tommy boy,' his mother said earnestly. 'You might be a big shot up in London, but down in Pontypridd you wipe your shoes when you come in, you're good to your wife, and you take your turn bringing in the coal.'

After years of wiggling at giggling miners in the homely bars and clubs of the Rhondda, and months of surviving on sausage butties and daydreams as just another poor hopeful in London, Tom had cracked it. The canny Gordon Mills, however, was already working out how to direct Tom away from One-Hit-Wondersville, and Tom's mother was keeping his feet on the ground. Family and friends celebrated 'It's Not Unusual''s chart-topping status at a Pontypridd pub, but Tom wasn't home for very long. He was soon to learn that as far as Gordon was concerned, travel not only broadens the mind but also lengthens the career.

The tour with Cilla Black had been Tom's first experience of fan fever. He was mobbed more than once by over-zealous females. In one town he had to slither free of his coat and leave them clutching it as he ran to safety.

But there were also benefits to making it... After years of being hard up, Tom finally had money to buy things. The first thing he bought was a car – a shiny new S-type Jaguar. Soon there came the first house – a huge contrast to living in the in-laws' basement. Early in '66, Tom, Linda and Mark moved into a dream home in Shepperton, Middlesex, near the Thames. For a mere eight grand, Tom got 'something bright, dashing, modern,

Inset: Tom and his mother Freda.

with plenty of room and lots of fresh air.' It also boasted a lounge with cream carpets, teak furniture and a long settee draped in orange and black Thai silk. Tiger Tom was purring. The mansion was approximately as big as the whole terrace he'd grown up in in Treforest. Even so, later the same year, it was too small for the aspirational singer – the garage wasn't big enough to house his new Rolls-Royce. The family moved a few miles up the river to a £25,000 home in Sunbury-on-Thames. Tom's never denied enjoying the more ostentatious trappings of stardom.

Money had come flying in thick and fast through the first year of success. For the American release of 'It's Not Unusual', in April '65, Gordon Mills accompanied Tom to the first of five TV performances on the popular, syndicated Stateside programme *The Ed Sullivan Show*. This constituted priceless exposure for the artist: The Beatles had famously used their appearance on the show as the launch pad for their 'conquering' of America. British beat music was in great demand there.

Yet the memory of Elvis's notorious pelvis, and some midWest resistance to rock 'n' roll – 'the devil's music' – persisted. Sullivan's producers were more than a touch conservative, and warned the new boy from Britain that unless he kept it cool, cameramen would only shoot his heated thrustings 'from the waist up'. Sensibly, Tiger Tom The Twisting Vocalist toned down his tigerish twisting just enough.

He couldn't, however, do anything to dilute his natural-born, soulful vocal prowess, which caused a sensation of its own. Radio listeners in the States had blithely assumed Tom was black, and countless black radio stations had set up interview time with him. Even when his management told them Tom was a white man, they laughed sceptically.

Tom met up with celebrated singer Dionne Warwick in New York, having been introduced to her previously in London. It was his first visit to the Big Apple, and she asked him what he'd like to see. Tom requested to be taken to the Harlem Apollo, in the sixties the centre of the Rhythm & Blues universe. There, Tom soon twigged he was the only white person in the place.

This wasn't the last time Tom was to be deemed an honorary 'soul man'. Throughout his career, great American soul singers have cited his name when asked which British vocalists they admire. Certainly, typical tight-buttoned English restraint has never been Tom's bag. You can take the boy out of Wales, but...

With 'It's Not Unusual' safely ensconced in the US Top Ten, and money at last in the bank, the Mills insisted that Tom and Linda join them for a brief holiday in the South of France. Mills clearly didn't want his new star to suffer from burn-out from his now-punishing schedule.

The tour with Cilla Black had been Tom's
first experience of fan fever.
He was mobbed more than once by
over-zealous females.

In one town he had to slither free of his coat and leave them clutching it as he ran to safety.

Returning to the ever-increasing demands and pressures of the pop life, such as purchasing new houses and cars, Tom concentrated on consolidating his position and sharpening up his image to keep apace with the changing times. Mills negotiated the minefield of press and publicity brilliantly. Meanwhile, The Squires weren't sure whether to go for it or grumble. While Tom was decorating his mansion, the lads were sharing a modest semi in Hounslow, still piling into a van together while Tom whizzed about in his Jag. The first signs of dissent emerged from within the ranks.

After a couple of water-treading hits, 'Once Upon A Time' and 'With These Hands' (later a favourite of Elvis's), a determined Tom had jutted and gyrated through a mammoth, coast-to-coast American tour organised by influential DJ Dick Clark, as well as mini-tours of numerous other countries. Then he was fortunate enough to be given a song to sing which all but matched the dazzling, quirky genius of 'It's Not Unusual'.

What's New Pussycat? has made its mark in the cinematic history books as the first film to feature Woody Allen in one of his own scripts. ('Twenty francs a week for helping the girls at the striptease dress and undress? That's not very much!' 'Hey, it's all I can afford.') He was way down the cast list, beneath Peter Sellers, Peter O'Toole, Capucine and Ursula Andress, in this 'swinging sixties' comedy of lust and lechery. These being themes which may have intrigued one Tom Jones, he was a natural choice to sing the title song.

Written by the musical maestros Burt Bacharach and Hal David, it was nominated for an Oscar for Best Song, and gave Tom another international top three smash. Its enormous, jovial refrain has been a household phrase ever since, whether with a dash of post-modern irony or in honest heartfelt homage. Nineties comedian Mike Myers, in full Austin Powers mode, performed a hilarious version in a 1998 Burt Bacharach tribute concert.

Although in '65 Bacharach had already written many of the greatest hit singles of all time, such as The Walker Brothers' 'Make It Easy On Yourself', Tom's good friend Dionne Warwick's 'Walk On By', Cilla Black's 'Anyone Who Had A Heart', Dusty Springfield's 'Wishin' And Hopin'' and The Shirelles' 'Baby It's You', he hadn't yet produced a film score worthy of his talents. *What's New Pussycat?* met that challenge, yielding not only the title song (pipped at the post for that Oscar by 'The Shadow Of Your Smile' from *The Sandpiper*), but 'Here I Am' for Dionne Warwick and 'My Little Red Book' for Manfred Mann (later an American hit for Arthur Lee's LA band Love).

The soundtrack album, re-released in 1999, offers in its sleeve notes the opinion that 'the choice of new Welsh heartthrob Tom Jones for the title track was an inspired one. Earlier in the year Jones had a hit with the brassy "It's Not Unusual", and a titillating post-Elvis lounge-rock sex symbol was born. He was the perfect voice and image for the romping title song, which shot to number three in the US...'

'He will break any heart without regret... his days of asking are all gone.'

It wasn't Tom's only movie-related magnum opus from '65. He also sang 'Thunderball', from the fourth and then-latest James Bond film, starring (of course) Sean Connery as 007. The film may have disappointed critics at the time, but its theme song, written by John Barry and Don Black, was another irresistible epic in the style of 'Goldfinger', which Tom sang as all-consumingly as only he could. 'They call him the winner who takes all,' he warned us intently. 'He will break any heart without regret... his days of asking are all gone...'

Perhaps Tom didn't have to do underwater battle with the forces of evil, but he did face other dangers. One being that, by possessing the talent and versatility to record such grand, ritzy, big production numbers, he invited accusations of 'selling out', given the period's obsession with rebellion and anti-establishment sentiments. 'True,' mused Tom, stung by a few printed criticisms, 'these ballads might be giving me a "square" image with the fans. What I'd really like is to release a big blues or R&B number, just to show everyone I can still do it, but my manager points out the snags to me and I think maybe he's right and I should stick to what I've been doing.' It was evident again that Gordon called the professional shots. 'I realise I'm becoming known as a film-song performer,' added Tom, 'and now I'm considering going into movies myself.' Although he'd had offers from Hollywood, he wanted to make his debut in a British film.

Life has a way of defying expectations, and much of what Tom said, with all the best intentions, fell by the wayside. Hopes of an acting career were ultimately to be awkwardly frustrated, and as for not leaving the country for long periods – well, Tom was soon earning so much that he was forced to become a tax exile.

In May 1966 Tom was recovering from having his tonsils out, relieved that the voice was standing up better than ever. He was back in love with America, announcing a month of Las Vegas shows for October. 'I follow Tony Bennett and Andy Williams into this new club, called Caesar's Palace,' he told reporters. He claimed the only member of his 'backing group' he could take with him was drummer Chris Slade (who'd improved vastly since the Welsh days, having taken copious lessons in London), and he'd be forming a new band out there. But postponements meant these shows didn't take place until the following spring, and at a different venue. Nevertheless, they were to prove life-altering, and career-defining, concerts.

The pinnacle of a busy, fizzy, '66 came, after nearly a year's absence from the charts, with the release of the single which was to become his most successful ever, and the only single that year to sell a million copies in Britain alone.

Tom is said to have found his best-known song on a Jerry Lee Lewis album called *Country Songs for City Folks*. The song, 'Green, Green Grass Of Home', became Tom's second British number one, and held on to the top slot for so long that newspapers ran articles about its extraordinary stamina. It also sold massively in America, and won respect from Nashville, the very heartland of country music. Tom had tentatively played his version of the song to his inspirational idol Jerry Lee Lewis, who, gratifyingly, had beamed and said it'd sell a million. He couldn't have foreseen it would sell far more than that.

Such a classic, old-school song ruffled the feathers of the burgeoning hippie movement. Indeed, *Melody Maker* dubbed it 'the song the hippies love to hate', adding that the sob story of 'that old oak tree that I used to play on' elicited 'a barrage of spleen from the self-appointed arbiters of teenage taste'.

He was about to take on America again. And this time he was serious.

Tom chuckled that criticism didn't worry him. 'I found the song for myself,' he said, 'so at least it's proved I can pick my own winners. It's also shown I can slow down a bit. I don't necessarily have to belt them out. I don't cater for the teenage screamers any more: I do polished shows.' Carefully, Tom, under Gordon's guidance, was moving, as he'd always been, towards career longevity. Tom accepted his gold disc for his biggest hit on stage, on television, on *Sunday Night at the London Palladium*.

One of Gordon's songs, 'Not Responsible', also proved popular for Tom that year, but it was 'Green, Green Grass Of Home', with its melancholy tale of love, homecomings and illusions, that a World Cup-winning nation took to its heart as an anthem. It struck an even greater chord in Wales, what with its title's echoes of the famed Richard Llewelyn novel about life in a tiny mining village, *How Green Was My Valley*. There was no longer any doubt: Tom Jones was the greatest living Welshman, an ambassador for the land of song. His confidence knowing no boundaries, he was about to take on America again. And this time he was serious.

Elvis was attending Tom's shows and, many said, copping a few of the Welshman's moves for his own comeback shows.

CHAPTER FIVE

FEVER, LAS VEGAS

Gordon Mills was a maestro at playing the media. Throughout 1967 'rumours' spread that Mills was in talks with the one and only Colonel Tom Parker, Elvis Presley's uber-manager (and perhaps something of a role model to Gordon). It was suggested that they were negotiating a deal whereby Parker, who'd been studying footage of Tom's live and TV performances, would handle Tom's career in America. It later transpired that the idea – again showing cool business savvy on Mills's part – was that Parker would advise Mills, and be available for consultation. Mills notionally welcomed the benefit of Elvis's svengali's experience and knowledge of the way things worked Stateside. It wasn't long before Elvis was attending Tom's shows and, many said, copping a few of the Welshman's moves for his own comeback shows.

'68 and '69 were to be Tom's Vegas years, years in which he dominated the American album charts while his glitzy but galvanised live shows entered the realms of folklore. The period began with music press reports that he was to pick up a then-astronomical million dollars for thirteen weeks' work for shows in Vegas and New York. 'It feels really, really great,' Tom told the *New Musical Express*, 'but the offer means more to me than the money itself – it shows they have real faith in me as an artist.' In preparation, he honed the act he'd been doing at London's Talk Of The Town, testing out new numbers.

Mills's wife Jo had once worked in Vegas as a Bluebell Girl, and her days of high-kicking had given her invaluable insight into the way the fame game worked in that city. When offers from smaller hotels and lounges poured in, Jo advised Gordon to turn them down, even if the money was tempting. She insisted that if Tom became known as a lounge act, he'd find it very hard to work his way up and cross over into major showroom stardom. She recommended they didn't settle for anything less than headlining. Tom had won rave reviews and receptions at New York's Copacabana and at Miami's Deauville, where the ritualistic wanton abandonment among otherwise sensible, mature females had caught on as a trend. (Little did even Mills realise how durable it was to prove.)

When Tom landed top billing at The Flamingo, it was something of a symbiotic marriage made in heaven. The Flamingo had seen better days, but a new management team, led by wonderfully named promoter Nick Naff, had just come in. Their hype techniques were second to none: Gordon for one could probably relate to these people.

Naff had coined the phrase 'Tom Jones Fever'. (It later lent itself to the title of the American album *The Tom Jones Fever Zone*. He placed bottles of 'Tom Jones fever pills' on every table. They wouldn't cure you, ran the spiel, but they'd keep the fever under some semblance of control. Radio commercials ran, informing the public what temperature Tom Jones fever was at that day. An ambulance waited ostentatiously at the rear of the concert hall, in case any frail fans passed out with the excitement of it all.

Perhaps it was a coincidence, perhaps it was another example of Mills's string-pulling, but at the same time as Tom Jones the singer arrived in Vegas, a 'sensual' stage show-cum-musical based on the film *Tom Jones*, which of course had inspired our hero's name, opened just along the Strip. This may at first have led to some confusion for eager punters, but not for long. If anything, it was an extra plug for the crooner. Soon the queues outside his show were getting longer and longer.

For the first few nights, Tom could walk through The Flamingo's lobby unmolested. After that, mobbing and hair-tearing became *de rigueur*. From that time, America's always perceived Tom Jones as one of the world's biggest superstars, and he in turn has perceived it, until very recently, as the country that's been kindest to him.

Gordon was realising more and more that career longevity for a singer meant appealing not just to pop-loving teenagers but to admirers in their twenties and thirties and beyond, admirers who had what's often comically referred to as 'disposable income'. Gordon would be very happy for Americans to dispose of this income in his and Tom's bank accounts.

Naff had transcended his name, and Tom Jones fever, if not utter hysteria, was growing daily. British journalist Alan Walsh wrote, under the headline 'Tom, toast of Vegas', that most of the big-name stars in Vegas during that spell had to be on-stage at the same time as Tom, but that Duke Ellington had gone out of his way to attend the opening night, and that a specially timed show was being organised to satisfy the demands of the temporarily local glitterati. 'It seems,' he added, 'that one of the stars in the audience will be Frank Sinatra, who is taking an interest in Tom's career.'

So was one Elvis Presley, and whereas on Tom's first US foray of '65 he'd been very much in awe of The King when meeting him, Elvis was now coming specifically to witness the Welshman in action. Nick Naff later said that when Elvis made his comeback in Vegas, he took those bits of Tom's performance that worked, and made them work for him.

Presley was a regular audience member as Tom's show next moved on, after eighteen euphoric months, to The International, a venue three times the size of The Flamingo, and the site where Elvis had made his comeback. Tom's reputation was now so phenomenal that he swiftly moved on again to Caesar's Palace. And when he played New York, one American critic gushed, 'Women screamed, stomped, went limp. Girls seemed to shudder with rapture. There was swinging Tom, doing the sort of things, pelvically speaking, that few fans will ever see...' (Those Copacabana shows broke Frank Sinatra's record for takings there, which had stood since the fifties.)

'Women screamed, stomped, went limp.
Girls seemed to shudder with rapture.
There was swinging Tom, doing the sort of things,
pelvically speaking, that few
fans will ever see...'

While Tom revelled in the Vegas showbiz lifestyle, drinking champagne till dawn and sleeping most of the day before throwing himself body and soul into another night's show, it was important he wasn't forgotten back home. Television was to prove vital. His *The Tom Jones Show* was screened prime-time in the UK, and was initially a huge success in the States too. Starting in February 1969, it was set to run three years, but was surprisingly dropped in January 1971, before its second season had ended. It had lost its hold in the top twenty, beaten in ratings battles by a popular detective programme of the time, *Ironside*.

The biggest acts in the world appeared on the shows, but they never upstaged Tom. And his effect on women was spectacular.

At its zenith, however, Tom's stature was staggering. When six shows were taped in LA, a record-breaking 30,000 applications for tickets flooded into the station, ABC. Funded by legendary, cigar-chomping impresario Lew Grade, *The Tom Jones Show* was a big-budget affair pulling in star guests from Tom's own hero Jerry Lee Lewis to Burt 'What's New Pussycat?' Bacharach. The list included such recording and movie-world giants as Janis Joplin, Johnny Cash, Cleo Laine, Perry Como, The Bee Gees, The Moody Blues and Raquel Welch. Such meetings gave Tom a great chance to display versatility from ballads to rockers and beyond, and of course the exposure in general was another, scarcely needed boost to his career and album sales.

Grade was paying Tom an enormous £9 million for the series, and trumpeting that the (originally intended) 80 shows would prove that Jones The Voice was without doubt 'the greatest singer in the world'. The biggest acts in the world appeared on the shows, but they never upstaged Tom. And his effect on women was spectacular.

Back in Blighty, the money was mounting up. Tom moved his wife and son from Sunbury-on-Thames to a gigantic mansion in Weybridge, having allocated the old Shepperton home to his parents. He also gave them a Ford Granada. His father therefore learnt to drive at the age of 56, so that he could zip back to South Wales whenever he

fancied. He wasn't averse to having a go behind the wheel of one of Tom's Rolls-Royces
or Mercedes Benz status symbols either.

Tom hadn't been a stranger to the British pop charts. 1967 was the year of two of
his most moving, melancholy hits, 'Detroit City' and the sublime 'I'm Coming Home',
co-written by the man who'd started the ball rolling, with Gordon, by co-writing 'It's Not
Unusual'. Les Reed was also partly responsible for the following year's smash, 'Delilah'.
This has since become a notorious karaoke favourite, and was years later covered by
The Sensational Alex Harvey Band. But Tom's full-throated version remains definitive, even
if his singing about a jealous man's heated vengeance against an unfaithful woman –
'I felt the knife in my hand, and she laughed no more... my my my Delilah, why why
why Delilah?' – was a nice slice of irony given his own frequent reputed strayings from the
marital straight and narrow. Another hit that year, the grand-chorused '(It Looks Like)
I'll Never Fall In Love Again', perhaps also demanded some willing suspension of disbelief.
Yet it boasts one of Tom's greatest vocal surges.

The *Delilah* album was one of Tom's most successful. His long players, such as
'67's covers hotch-potch *Smash Hits* or his common live recordings, rarely really captured
the essence of Tom, but he usually had one sitting comfortably in the Top Ten in the years
between '66 and '71. *Delilah*, which also included 'I'm Coming Home', 'The Rose' and
'Things I Wanna Do', shunted The Small Faces from the top of the album charts for
one week in September '68. The single of the same name, surprisingly, was thwarted at
number two.

*Thomas and Freda Woodward
with the car Tom bought them, outside
the house in which he was born.*

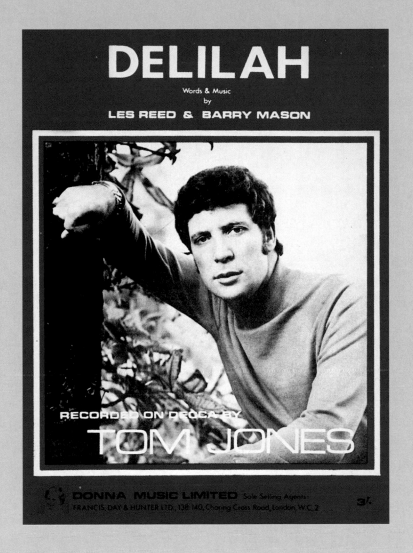

At times in '69 he had five or six different albums in the US charts simultaneously.

The end of the sixties saw Tom grinning like the proverbial Cheshire cat as he prowled the arena of showbiz, undisputed champion of his several genres. He'd worked for it. Marathon American tour schedules had earned him gargantuan sums of money, while at times in '69 he had five or six different albums in the US charts simultaneously.

The Squires, however – remember them? – were not so happy. For them, 'Tom Jones fever' was about to well and truly break. While four years' touring as 'the backing band'

'I never worry, because I always know that Tom is coming home.'

CHAPTER SIX

NOT RESPONSIBLE

Lusty Tom's durable sexual charisma is denied by none. His 'actual' sexual exploits, however, have been reported, glamorised, denied and counter-denied. Over the best part of four decades, newspapers have enjoyed spreading rumour and scandal on an almost weekly basis. Tom's had his fair share of flings and then some, as he's admitted – cheerily as often as wearily. Apparently with well-known soul divas, with publicity-crazed Miss Worlds, and with 'he used me as a plaything' kiss-and-tellers out to make a killing. Yet whether none or all of the stories are true, Tom remains – happily, it would appear – married to Linda, mother of his current manager. After over 40 years. Something about the old Welsh devil likes the notion of eternal wedlock, while something in Linda has been strong enough to disregard the constant gossip.

Tom's alleged dirty dalliances began to make front-page news in the mid-sixties, when he was consolidating his status as one of the world's biggest and best-paid superstars and sex symbols. In 1969 the normally reclusive Linda agreed to an interview with the *Daily Mirror*, wherein – sitting in their twenty-room mansion – she reassured any concerned parties that, 'I never worry, because I always know that Tom is coming home.

I am sure of him.' Linda, clearly content to not be sewing stockings at £4 a week any longer, laughed, 'There are some girls who are pretty frank in what they say... how they'd like to go to bed with him and so on. But mainly they're nice, and tell me how lucky I am. Well, I know I'm lucky – it's like a dream. It's just that I prefer to stay at home while Tom does all the talking.'

There was an interesting exchange later in this interview. Eleven-year-old Mark said, 'I don't know what I want to do when I leave school. I haven't made up my mind.' Linda, revealingly, and contrarily to the popular public perception, added, 'I'd like him to go into show business in some way. He's grown up with records.' How very prophetic those words were to prove.

'There he was, dressed in a ruffled white shirt, black tuxedo and, of course, skin-tight trousers. Sparks flew! He was gorgeous.'

Mary Wilson

'I love Tom's records too,' Linda concluded. 'Even if he wasn't my husband, I'd still go out and buy them. He's a very loving man. All that a woman could ask for.'

It seems that Linda, however, was not the only woman who thought so. In 1967 Tom had met Mary Wilson, of the massively acclaimed and influential group The Supremes. Later, in her autobiography *Dreamgirl*, she wrote of their passionate affair. Tom could hardly fail to be attracted to a woman whose fame and glamour quotients at the time equalled his own.

Her breathy words on that first encounter, on tour in Munich, express a certain headiness. 'There he was, dressed in a ruffled white shirt, black tuxedo and, of course, skin-tight trousers. Sparks flew! He was gorgeous. Why had I waited so long?'

Wilson, whose book also tells of affairs with actor Steve McQueen and film mogul David Puttnam, had to wait a little longer, as that night Tom Jones was accompanying Richard Burton and Elizabeth Taylor to a function. But subsequent long conversations with Mary Wilson led to a relationship which she declared showed him to be 'a great friend in addition to being a fine lover'. Yet when she – eventually – learnt he was married with a son, she was stunned. 'Tom was married! I couldn't believe it! Maybe he figured that since every other woman in the Western world knew that he was 'unavailable', I should too... I resolved to break it off the next time I saw him, but when that time came I realised I couldn't. It was too late.'

The demise of the affair, however, was inevitable. 'Ironically,' Wilson wrote, 'Tom's devotion to his wife was one of the things I admired most about him. Never once did he even hint he'd leave her, but I couldn't let go. Sometimes I was so foolish, going so far as to telephone his home in England, only to hang up when his wife answered.'

Mary's book also relates that she and Tom would leave coded phone messages for each other, saying that 'Jimi Hendrix called'. 'We'd laugh and talk and just be so happy together,' she went on. 'I didn't care what anyone thought. I was young and in love.'

Despite the semi-secrecy, this romance did threaten Tom's marriage. The couple were sharing a rented love nest in, of all places, Bournemouth, when in the summer of 1968 an angry Linda telephoned, suspicions aroused if not inflamed. By Wilson's account, a panic-stricken Tom packed Wilson off to London in a Limo. Linda arrived and searched the house, but any traces of infidelity had been hurriedly tidied away. Yet when she discovered a meal still simmering in the oven, she knew better than to fall for the improvised excuse of Tom, who never cooked, that his road manager was the chef responsible. She's apparently given Tom hell about the affair many times since.

So Tom was compelled to end the romance. In Wilson's book she concedes that he broke it off, telling her at her Hollywood home that it wasn't fair to her, that there was no future in it. She agreed, knowing he was never going to leave his wife. When, some time later, he took Linda backstage with him after a Supremes concert, she knew for sure that the game was up. Before long she was married herself, and when her own husband cheated on her, felt a pang of remorse. She concluded, 'Still, Tom remains one of the very special people in my life.' Of the revelations in *Dreamgirl*, Jones was to later chuckle to an interviewer, 'That was like getting caught out twice!'

Here was a red-blooded Welsh seducer, rising to giddy heights of fame as a walking, gyrating piece of sexual mythology, in the late sixties.

This was by no means the singer's only reported fling with a high-profile woman from the world of showbiz and entertainment. Once he was encamped in America for most of his time, he found them all but beating down his backstage door. Here was a red-blooded Welsh seducer, rising to giddy heights of fame as a walking, gyrating piece of sexual mythology, in the late sixties, in arguably the most liberated continent.

The after-show, all-night parties were riddled with willing groupies, and if they could stay up all night while Tom drank, they were in with a chance of bagging their desired prize. Manager Gordon Mills, legend has it, gave Tom a run for his money as chief Lothario.

It wasn't unknown for Tom, the pop star, to send a bodyguard or member of his touring entourage over to a woman in a club or party to invite them to join Tom and his circle. This required the bare minimum of effort from Tom, but apparently yielded a high success ratio.

Tellingly for Tom, a flirtation with Diana Dors led to nothing because, as Dors told it, she intimidated him. Her brassy humour and confidence played on his macho insecurities.

The affair which gleaned the most publicity, however, was a melodramatic series of meetings in 1973 with Marjorie Wallace, then the recently crowned Miss World. The tabloids of the era lapped this affair up, especially as it involved at various points a surreal number of other famous, or infamous, male sex symbols.

Wallace was known to be the regular girlfriend of Peter Revson, a successful, eligible, racing-car driver. However, at the celebratory ball after the Miss World contest, Chris Hutchins, Gordon Mills's press liaisons officer (and therefore promoter of not only Tom Jones but also ascendant crooner Engelbert Humperdinck), spotted Wallace dancing with boxer Joe Bugner. Determined to go one better, he persuaded Humperdinck to hog the next day's front pages instead. A kiss ensued between the former Gerry Dorsey and the new Miss World. Humperdinck invited Wallace to his London Palladium show that week, but any romantic dabblings were purely cosmetic, and engineered by Hutchins.

'Everywhere he goes he is chased by women.'

A month later, however, the eager Wallace was at the Palladium again, this time to see Tom Jones in action. They spent time alone together backstage, and it's been reported that they went back to his hotel suite for the night.

In the press, even Tom's mother-in-law, Linda's mother Vi, was interviewed about this in her (Tom-bought) Glamorgan home. 'Who isn't after Tommy?' she asked. 'Everywhere he goes he is chased by women. Miss Wallace is just one of the crowd. She means nothing to Tommy. There's only one girl in Tommy's life, and that's Linda. He only has eyes for her. Linda's not a bit worried about the tales of Tommy and this Wallace girl.'

Protesting too much? Soon after this, presumably with the Mills/Hutchins publicity drive switching horses midstream, the pair 'officially' met, on the set of the perhaps appropriately named BBC extravaganza *Tom Jones On Happiness Island*. On the show, filmed in Barbados, Tom sang the Bread ballad '(I Want To) Make It With You' to the enchanted beauty queen, finishing it with the flourish of a passionate kiss. This was witnessed by millions of viewers, despite the best damage limitation efforts of Julia Morley, who ran Miss World and therefore Wallace's public image.

Tom then took off on a brief concert tour of Holland, but Marjorie, back in London, couldn't stay out of the headlines for long. She was snapped cavorting out and about with the Irish maverick footballing legend and "fifth Beatle," not to mention dedicated womaniser, George Best. But this fling was to end in tears and recriminations:

Tom Jones, after a New York court-ordered blood test. Her son Jonathan, born in '88, was alleged to have been born of a five-day fling when the singer played a week of shows in New York, during which time Berkery claimed they were rarely apart. Jones was ordered to pay £2,000 per month for the boy's upkeep. Berkery said she'd never known Tom was married, and was doing this not for the money, but 'for the principle. It's heartless for a man not to acknowledge his own son. He's a loathsome human being, who just used me for sex.'

The *Mail On Sunday* reported that the young boy 'repeatedly sings "What's New Pussycat?", "Green, Green Grass Of Home" and "Delilah" into a toy microphone.' By '98, his mother was taking him to see a Tom Jones concert in Florida, telling the papers she was 'not sure yet whether to go backstage'.

Indeed, the nineties, despite Tom's reaching an age when most men struggle to find the energy to ask what Viagra is, have seen no let-up in the stream of Sunday tabloid scandals concerning his alleged frisky frolics and dirty dalliances. The decade began with the ever-concerned *News of the World* running a 1991 'exclusive' headlined 'Missus Catches Tom Canoodling With Lover'.

Evidently, Linda had threatened Tom with divorce after 33 years of marriage. She'd turned a blind eye, as so often, to his ten-month affair with 'leggy, 21-year-old student' Cindy Montgomery, but when she caught them in the act at his LA mansion, hit the (expensive) roof. Tom took cover in a nearby hotel, waiting for the heat to die down.

'This time he's gone too far,' said 'a friend'. 'Linda's mortified that he sneaked the girl into their home.' The story told how Tom had fallen for the girl after being introduced, in a nice irony, by her mother. He'd whisked her off to Hawaii, Las Vegas and New York for 'romantic' weekends, and she'd been his companion as he rehearsed in London for a British tour. An intriguing coda to the tale had Linda's sister Rosalyn denying the allegations. In fact, she said, Cindy didn't even exist – 'Cindy Montgomery' was a jocular nickname used by the crew for Tom's bodyguard, Chris Montgomery. The 'incriminating' photos? Just Tom kindly posing with another adoring fan. On the same page it was reported that Linda also denied that Tom had ever slept with Katherine Berkery.

Mr Montgomery, by now Tom's ex-minder, turned out to be less fiercely loyal later that year, telling the same newspaper that the sex symbol was no longer the licentious legend of folklore. 'In the old days he could have any girl he fancied, but now it's a case of taking what's offered. The old fire has definitely died down quite a bit.'

Montgomery followed up with tell-tale anecdotes about Tom and an air hostess all but joining the mile-high club, Tom's leanings towards voyeurism and porn movies, his use of Listerine to revive his worn-out manhood, and Tom's preference for 'big' girls,

'I shall never regret what's happened to me, except perhaps for not seeing the green, green grass of home as often as I'd have liked.'

CHAPTER SEVEN

THE WELSH PRINCE OF BEL AIR

Back in January of 1969, the *Observer* both glorified and satirised Tom Jones's meteoric rise to the top rungs of the showbiz ladder. It revealed that when he first appeared at the London Palladium in '67, a troupe of performing elephants shared the bill. And that in '63, this scandal-magnet of a man had filled in at short notice for another performer who'd been unavoidably detained. Her name was Mandy Rice-Davies.

'Green-eyed Tiger Tom,' opined the broadsheet, 'appeals to the maturer woman. What with his George Raft sideburns and Sicilian Sunday suit, this self-confessed ex-drunkard, ex-Teddy boy and ex-mini-gangster, who used to wear a ring in the shape of a skull and crossbones, roared around the stage like some bubbling Quatermass monster, seizing every song by the scruff of the neck, rattling it about and, eventually, choking it to death.'

Inset: Tom and Engelbert pose

with a Rolls-Royce.

Tom might have taken offence at some of this. That bit about being an 'ex' drunkard, at least.

The article went on that Tom's new television show was costing a cool three grand per minute, and that he'd sold no less than 26 million records in the four years since 'It's Not Unusual'. 'Vocally, he's a rabble-rouser. In days when nice little pop singers are still mods, he is unashamedly a rocker. He is the mum's Mick Jagger, the performing bear of the middle-class audience. And for those who can't understand or don't want to know about the more subtle happenings of pop, the no-nonsense corn of Jones the miner's son has an immediate and obvious appeal.'

When 'Green, Green Grass Of Home' was at number one, the Top Ten had included – as well as Gene Pitney, The Seekers and Val Doonican – such acts as The Beach Boys ('Good Vibrations'), The Small Faces ('My Mind's Eye'), Manfred Mann ('Semi-Detached Suburban Mr James') and The Kinks ('Dead End Street'). Asked about his chart contemporaries' fans, Tom snarled, 'When I see them squatting with their banners in their sandals, I feel like telling them to get off their backsides and do something. They do nothing. They're bums.'

Just to crown the surrealism, this piece climaxed with the information that, upstairs in his house, Tom kept a dozen guns, and 50 or 60 knives. Oh, and some swords.

If Tom had known he was going to spend so much of his time in America, he's always sworn, he'd have taken more of Wales with him. He'd have had his old house moved over there, brick by brick, and bought the old double-decker bus he used to ride. 'How,' he once asked, 'can you possibly compare the lush, green Rhondda Valley with the sandswept, arid humidity of Las Vegas, Nevada? You can't. But Vegas has become my second home because of work...

'I shall never regret what's happened to me,' he added, 'except perhaps for not seeing the green, green grass of home as often as I'd have liked.'

Even by 1969, Tom and Gordon, and by now Gordon's other successful singing discovery, Engelbert Humperdinck, had been earning enough to move to salubrious St George's Hill in Weybridge, where John Lennon, Paul McCartney, and Cliff Richard had bought homes at various times. The three new residents lived within a mile of each other, Gordon renaming his mansion Little Rhondda. Tom's was named Torpoint. He enjoyed his very own security force, swimming pool and gymnasium complex.

To battle the Inland Revenue's demands, the trio set up a company, MAM, and traded on the stock market. Gordon was becoming a businessman par excellence. His record label's first release, 'I Hear You Knocking' by Dave Edmunds, went to number one in 1970.

WIth Glen Campbell, 1970.

(He later nurtured another chart-topping young star, one Raymond O'Sullivan. Gordon changed his name to Gilbert. Tom sold him a Mercedes.)

Gordon, Tom and Engelbert shared a jet, costing them three-quarters of a million pounds. They hardly used it. But when Labour came into government in '74, Tom figured his high earnings meant his taxes accounted for between 80 and 90 per cent of his income. He was forced to juggle his time between Britain and America as a means of financial damage limitation. He'd bought a huge farm in Sussex with his MAM co-directors, but couldn't afford to visit the UK long enough to see it. To see even his wife and son, he had to meet them in 'neutral territory' such as France or Belgium. Son Mark began to spend time on the road with Tom.

So in 1974 Tom had to buy a permanent home in America. For a million dollars, he purchased Dean Martin's former estate in LA's staggeringly expensive Bel Air. (Seven years later it was worth seven times that amount.) 'This house is just like me,' Tom told the *Observer* years later. 'Conceived in 1939 and finished in 1940.' He also soon bought Beverly Hills houses for his parents and sister, and for Mark and his new American wife Donna.

The sixteen-room, red-brick Bel Air home was to be gilded by Welsh dragons on its high gates. Its swimming pool was vast, the largest in Bel Air. The red brick, uncommon in the area because it was susceptible to earthquakes, gave its owner a reassuring hint of Britishness. The furniture was shipped over from Torpoint. Tom's gold records adorned the halls. An extension housing a screening room-cum-theatre opened out on to the pool. The flower beds bloomed opulently with African palms, camelias, hibiscus, oleanders and bougainvillaeas. And that red telephone box sat incongruously among these gardens. Most importantly, perhaps, Tom got his Green Card, and settled for the more favourable American tax system. Linda was persuaded to join her exiled husband.

The grounds were soon to be coloured by toy trains and jeeps for Alexander, Mark's son and Tom's grandson, born in '83, and a priceless fountain flown in from Italy. 'When I play with my grandson,' said Tom, 'it reminds me of what life's all about.' In '87, granddaughter Emma joined the family.

Gordon Mills also moved to the States, although estranged wife Jo remained in Weybridge. Mills couldn't take all of his private zoo with him, and so donated seven orang-utans and five gorillas to the San Diego Zoo. This explains why the first baby gorilla born in California for twenty years was named Gordon.

Eventually, disagreements over money and professional rivalry led to Engelbert Humperdinck leaving Gordon and Tom's organisation. For his part, Humperdinck has always been at pains to stress since that his problem was with Gordon as a manager,

not Tom as a person. After Gordon's sad death in the mid-eighties, the two singers said they were still friends, though Humperdinck felt too awkward to attend Mills's funeral. (By then, Gilbert O'Sullivan had successfully sued Mills for mismanagement, claiming several million pounds from sales of his records had unjustly gone to MAM rather than to him. He won, and won big.)

Meanwhile, Tom, who so pined for his fatherland that he kept HP sauce on the table, was compensated by his own accumulated wealth. 'I could never have done it by staying at home,' he told the *Daily Express* on a visit to Wales in 1983. 'Depending on how you look at it, you can blame or credit Harold Wilson with my success abroad. I was touring in the States when Labour unexpectedly won the '74 election, and Gordon frantically called me, saying, "Don't come back! The Labour government will tax you out of existence!" 'The laugh was, coming from a family of coalminers, we always voted Labour. No question about it. But my old dad, who died two years ago, said that if voting Tory would get his boy home, he'd do it. And he did, which my mam still can't quite believe...'

'I don't like the hand I've been forced to play, but what can I do about it? I love Britain and love living there — it's home — but I've been forced into exile.'

On Tom's father's death from emphysema in '81, aged 72, all the papers reported that the singer locked himself in his home and cried for a week. Tom's money had at least allowed him to retire from the mines early, and to experience such absurdities as meeting Elvis and Sinatra. And he'd often popped out to a British-style pub in Santa Monica for a quick pint with Tom Junior.

Tom would often reiterate to the press how he hadn't wanted to turn his back on Britain. In '76, under the headline 'Why I'm Quitting The Green, Green Grass Of Home', he moaned to the *People*, 'I've been forced into exile and I don't like it one little bit.' He denounced British taxmen: 'They really are a shower. They're cutting their own throats and they don't seem to realise it. Let's say I make two million dollars this year — the government would take about 98 per cent of that if I lived at home. Now I don't mind paying taxes, but 98 per cent is just ridiculous. There's no incentive for me to earn large amounts of bread if it's all going to be eaten by the taxman.

At this point still waiting for his Green Card, Tom went on, 'I don't like the hand I've been forced to play, but what can I do about it? I love Britain and love living there – it's home – but I've been forced into exile.

The *Express* reported another landmark in '83. At Caesar's Palace, Tom had picked up from the stage the 5,000th room key tossed up there by a female admirer. It was ceremoniously framed and mounted in the hotel's lobby. Quite who had been so accurately keeping count was not revealed. Asked if he'd ever used one of these keys, Tom laughed, 'No, honest! I mean, you never bloody well know what you might find on the other side of the door.' Returning to a recurring theme, he went on, 'My wife isn't the jealous type. She asks no questions, so I tell no lies. That's the way it is.'

But by the late eighties, Linda, who didn't like Hollywood's glitz and glamour, was urging a tanned Tom to move back to Britain. Tom explained that she'd become a lonely, homesick recluse, making no friends in the States, refusing to drive or take taxis or meet new people who Tom fancied inviting round. 'She's got a real problem about meeting people,' he told the *News of the World*. 'The only thing she likes about my job is the money I earn, but that's meaningless when it doesn't make you happy. What she wants now is to come home, so that's what she'll have. I always do what she tells me. She never puts up with any b*llsh*t from me. I love that: what she says goes.'

'To her I'm no star, I'm Tom from the next street in Wales.'

He went on to make a fair point. 'You see so many showbiz marriages fail – the guy becomes successful and the missus gets the push. But there's no way that will ever happen to us. She knows me inside out – to her I'm no star, I'm Tom from the next street in Wales.'

But when Linda stayed in Wales after visiting family at Christmas '88, Tom's work commitments took him back to California. (And that's pretty much the way it's been since, although in the nineties papers reported that Tom was on the verge of returning full-time to the UK, the Californian tax system having radically altered.) So Linda moved into a seven-bedroomed mansion (tennis courts, entertainment complex, duck ponds) named Llwynddu House, in Welsh St Donats in the beautiful Vale of Glamorgan. Tom's luxurious home was just 7,000 miles away.

I came over just for a holiday – but fell in love with Wales all over again,' Linda told the *Mirror*. 'I'm a very happy woman with a wonderful husband. We love each other just as much as ever – that's for the record.'

'Linda decided that when I'm on the road, she'd rather be in Wales than LA,' said Tom. 'It's the lesser of two evils. She's with people she grew up with there.' Tom kept his American residency, using both his Green Card and his British passport. The glamour and glitz, and hobnobbing with equally big superstars, seemed a delight to him, not a hassle as they did to his wife. In Wales, she apparently spends much of her time scanning market stalls for bargains with her sister. Pontypridd is just across the valleys.

'So I spend a lot of time on the road,' Tom shrugged to the British press. 'But when I go home our love life is fresh. Maybe if I was always there it would be stale.'

If America was attractive to Tom for many reasons, he readily agreed that he always felt safer in Britain. America held the danger of kidnappers, assassins and all-round general crazies. Though his fitness training regime was as arduous as ever, he admitted to carrying a handgun, an idea given to him by Elvis Presley, and worried about his grandchildren's well-being. In '92 he told the *People* magazine, 'You have to be aware that you're vulnerable. In the States especially, you have to have high security. Elvis once gave me a pistol as a present – he carried a gun everywhere. Even on stage he used to conceal it in the small of his back.'

'I was brought up on light ale, and I've always believed that pop is better than pot.'

Tom wasn't being paranoid, entirely. In '69 he'd learnt that, to his understandable horror, his name, along with Frank Sinatra's and Liz Taylor's, had been on the gruesome hit list of Charles Manson's psychotic followers.

'Apparently the plan was that a girl from his gang would come to one of my concerts, somehow get close to me afterwards, and then try to kill me while giving me one. In the moment of ecstasy. I tell you, as far as messing around goes, something like that puts a block on any thoughts in that area.

'It was real scary. Manson was an aspiring songwriter and he was jealous of anyone successful. I suppose he thought if he killed us all he'd stand a better chance.'

After that, Tom's security systems had been seriously stepped up. The LA house he bought from Dean Martin used to have live-in security guards, but Tom couldn't live like that. So Tom built a huge wall around the grounds to deter intruders, and installed panic buttons linked directly to the police.

But like John Lennon,' he pondered, 'if anyone really wanted to do something, I couldn't stop them.'

An hour a day in the gym helped Tom's peace of mind, not to mention his legendary hirsute physique. And one frequent superstar lifestyle accessory was abhorred by the working class hero: while a big drinker, he's always been staunchly anti-drugs.

'I love what I do and I wouldn't want anything to get in the way of it,' he's said. 'That's why I've always avoided drugs. I was brought up on light ale, and I've always believed that pop is better than pot. With the occasional drink, you can consume it and not show it. Whereas with drugs, perfectly normal people are reduced to blithering idiots within minutes. Seeing people take drugs upsets me.' Tom was often known to walk out of a club or party immediately if he saw drugs in the vicinity. 'I've been at showbiz parties in very respectable London hotels where I've been the only one drinking and everyone else is on drugs,' he went on. 'You can't be a performer and do drugs, I reckon. I remember the bass player in one of my early band line-ups trying pot for the first time then going to pieces on stage. He was simply incapable of playing. Now if he'd been drunk, we could've propped him up against a wall and he could still have played. But he was all over the place; couldn't even change chords. That shocked me.'

When his friend Elvis Presley indulged, Tom had no sympathy. Ironically, Presley had been appointed an official narcotics agent by President Richard Nixon. 'Elvis,' Tom snapped, 'should have arrested himself.'

'I'll be around until the green, green grass
is turned into a car park.'

CHAPTER EIGHT

SAY GOODBYE TO HOLLYWOOD

Asked about career longevity in 1987, Tom mused, 'Regarding my voice and work, Frank Sinatra told me back in '67 that I'd never last if I didn't change the way I sang. That my voice would go.' He paused. 'But what other way is there?' He laughed. 'I'll be around until the green, green grass is turned into a car park.'

Tom may eventually have become a touch blasé about meeting Sinatra and countless other major league celebrities, but his relationship with Elvis Presley, which became a genuine friendship, meant a great deal to him – indeed to both men. Elvis had been one of Tom's prime idols back in Britain, while the Welshman's phenomenally successful Vegas seasons helped to precipitate and inspire Elvis's own comeback shows of the late sixties.

Back on an early American visit, in '65, it had been arranged for rising star Tom to be granted a brief meeting with The King at LA's Paramount Studios, where Presley was filming one of his many indifferent movies. Tom nervously hovered beside the set, until Colonel Tom Parker beckoned him over between scenes. Tom was thrilled at Elvis's approach.

'He walked towards me singing "With These Hands". I couldn't believe it! Not only that, he knew every track on my album. He asked me how I sang like that, coming from Wales.' Tom was proud and amazed. 'There I was, ready to tell him how much he'd influenced me, and he began telling me how much he liked my records!'

Later in the decade, Tom was less of a great white hope and more of a conquering hero, while Elvis was planning to emerge, at Vegas, from a lull in his career. He asked Tom's promoters if he could watch his show quietly, without anyone knowing, before being reintroduced. He sat in the shadows and watched Tom intently.

'There I was, ready to tell him how much he'd influenced me, and he began telling me how much he liked my records!'

As the two bonded over time, Tom would lecture Elvis about drug use and Elvis would confide in Tom about his battles to control his weight. Elvis famously often sang 'Delilah' as a dressing-room warm-up. One anecdote Tom later told involved Elvis going backstage to see Tom as the Welshman was showering after a concert. They conversed as Tom washed, and Elvis used the nearby toilet. His lace-up tight leather trousers then proved problematical, however, and Presley had to call for an assistant to help him tie them up again. Another time Tom reported that Elvis used to blow up televisions by shooting them.

Tom's said he felt 'closer to him than to any other entertainer.' The two often discussed the movie world, and the difficulties of a singer finding decent roles in films. In '92 Tom conceded, 'I've never made a movie because the parts I'm offered never have any meat in them. I've always been offered these Elvis-type roles and, believe me, Elvis hated them himself. The only thing that would've appealed to me would've been a part like one of The Wild Bunch. So I'll just stick to singing. Anyway, I've only ever wanted to rock.'

Not strictly true: Tom and his management had put much effort into trying to get film projects off the ground earlier in his career. Though he was to win some acclaim for his game gyrations (as himself) in director Tim Burton's 1996 sci-fi caper *Mars Attacks!*, he'd hoped Hollywood would beckon much earlier.

From the mid-sixties, when he'd recorded the theme songs to *What's New Pussycat?* and *Thunderball*, newspapers had linked him with blockbusters, but the right part never materialised. In '68, Tom had announced, 'I want to do films. I want audiences to recognise me.' Always one to expand his share of the commercial market, Gordon Mills had been equally keen.

With the success of Tom's concerts, records and television shows, cinema seemed the next logical step. In '71 he said, 'I've been a bit frightened, and stayed away from films – I don't want people to say, "Oh, he's not such a good actor." But I'm making a film in October.' Jones and Mills had bought the film rights to a novel, *The Gospel Singer*, by the controversial writer Harry Crews. Published in '68, it had garnered rave reviews and a cult following. So late in '71, United Artists announced they'd signed the singer to a three-movie deal. *The Gospel Singer* was being adapted for the screen already. Charlene Tilton, known for her role as Miss Lucy in TV series *Dallas*, was tipped to co-star. 'Between them,' roared the press, 'they're bound to set the temperature soaring.'

This all proved too good to be true – a man who'd never acted was being given a superstar's Hollywood contract. Yet Tom's hopes never reached fruition. The decade was spent in legal arguments and 'development hell'. Tom got cold feet about playing a character – an inspirational South Georgia gospel singer who falls prey to corruption and is lynched by his former followers – who might offend the sensibilities of the Bible Belt states. There were attempts to change the ending of the story, as it involved Tom's death on camera, and Tom also made it clear that he was not enamoured of dyeing his hair blond for the role. Harry Crews did, however, admit that Jones could fake a great Southern accent. Tom later revealed that Elvis had been his voice coach.

Elvis famously often sang 'Delilah' as a dressing-room warm-up.

While the on-off saga dragged on, other offers came Tom's way. In '76 he was approached about a part in *The Stud*, a sexploitation frolic wherein he would have played Joan Collins' lover. (The part later went to Oliver Tobias.) Again, Tom and his advisers thought the subject matter too risky; too near the knuckle. He complained that the material was just short of pornographic, conveniently failing to see any link between this and his knicker-strewn stage act.

It was later rumoured that another novel by Jackie Collins, author of *The Stud* and sister of Joan, was based on Tom's raunchy on-the-road exploits. *Lovers and Gamblers* featured a promiscuous rock star who liked threesomes, and whose shy son travelled with him on tour...

Yet another mooted film project, *Yockowald*, became bogged down in ifs, buts and maybes. Tom was tipped to play a non-singing, 'flamboyant, extroverted, hired assassin.' The film had an experienced producer and director behind it, and Tom cancelled eleven weeks of lucrative Nevada bookings, incurring the wrath of righteous promoters, in order to learn his lines. He hadn't had a hit single for some time (since, in fact, 1971's 'She's A Lady'), and while money was still pouring in thanks to MAM, he coveted a new boost to his professional profile. But after just three weeks of shooting, the project hit unanticipated financial catastrophes.

A shame, as Tom had been profoundly enthused. 'I play a sort of unsophisticated James Bond,' he told the *People*. 'I'm an undercover agent for the CIA who looks like a bum and is always hustling, playing poker, shooting dice ... getting leads from the people living in the ghetto.

'I really dig this movie-making business. It's very demanding and different from other stuff I've done. When I was shooting my weekly TV show they'd use four cameras at once to get the various angles. In a movie you're generally only using one, and it takes time and patience on my part, the director's, and the other actors', to shoot and reshoot the necessary angles. I haven't done a lot of dialogue yet, but the director's told me he's very pleased with the daily rushes. I couldn't have wished for a better director and friend – he knows, of course, that this is my first movie, and he's really helping me along with everything.'

The *People* story continued: 'His next scene then goes without a hitch, and the director says it's a wrap on the first take. Tom proudly sits down in his large canvas director's chair and, with a wink, points to his name on the back. It's as if to say, "See, I've arrived. At last, I'm a movie star."'

The collapse of this project, then, and with it Tom's ambitions in that direction, was an inexplicable stroke of rotten luck (not often encountered in Tom's career). 'The role fitted him like a glove,' the producer was to say. The backing bank had been suddenly sold to Japanese investors, who allowed the project to fall by the wayside. Tom was bewildered, and anxious; at 38, time wasn't, in this area, on his side.

Gordon and Tom became pro-active. They built a recording studio in Hollywood and started a film production company. On the movie front they set their sights more modestly, and Tom signed to play a roguish but charming singer with a sideline in smuggling in an NBC television movie, *Pleasure Cove*.

Seen as a kind of cross between two popular TV shows, *The Love Boat* and *Fantasy Island*, this pilot never made it as far as becoming a series. Bikinis and margaritas were its props. Everyone involved reckoned Tom was more than competent, and easy to work with, but after screening in January '79, the film was soon forgotten. A cousin told Tom, 'If I was you, I'd stick to singing.'

He did, but not before contradicting his earlier zeal. 'I'm not a frustrated actor, nothing like that,' he said. 'In fact, I've always looked on acting as hard work, and now, after *Pleasure Cove*, I know that's true.'

In '89 Tom was 'awarded' a star on Hollywood Boulevard's Walk Of Fame, but this was little more than a cheesy promotional stunt, chiefly bought and paid for (at merely $3,500) by his devoted fan club.

As himself, Tom cheerily sang and swung as the planet exploded.

Happily, with Tom's return to credibility and fashion in the nineties, *Mars Attacks!* gained him fleets of new fans, and captured something of Jones The Voice and Jones The Icon on big-screen celluloid. Helmed by the mischievous director of some of the Batman films, and such sinister modern fairy tales as *Edward Scissorhands*, it was based on the notoriously violent and graphic children's picture cards of 1962. Pitched manically between spoof comedy and full-on gore, it saw a Martian invasion of earth punctuating mass killings of humans with quirky jokes and deranged flirtations. The cast was stellar enough to do Tom justice, including as it did his friend Jack Nicholson as a gullible American president, Glenn Close, Annette Bening, Sarah Jessica Parker, Pierce (James Bond) Brosnan, Pam Grier, Danny De Vito, Michael J. Fox and Rod Steiger. As himself, Tom cheerily sang and swung as the planet exploded. Well, what else would he do?

On stage in Vegas – of course – he's startled as Martians join his band midway through a grinding 'It's Not Unusual'. His response? 'Jesus Christ!' He scarpers backstage, where he hooks up with two fellow scarperers, boxer Jim Brown and hippie Annette Bening. 'Hell of a punch,' he tells Brown when the heavyweight floors an invader. 'Saw you fight in Cardiff Wales once.' Tom's asked if he can fly a plane. 'Sure.' He shrugs manfully. 'You got one?'

Tom flies Bening to safety, and the planet is rescued by the Martians' adverse reactions to the sounds of Slim Whitman. Our indestructible hero is, tellingly, one of the few survivors of the planet's near-annihilation: as a new hopeful day breaks, he's seen standing godlike on a cliff top above the sea, one hand holding an eagle, the other on a baby deer. We hear the intro to 'It's Not Unusual', Tom feels the rhythm and kicks in, and the film finishes. He's the last man standing. Now that's cool, cinematic mythology.

In '98, however, the myth wobbled. Filming a cameo role in Dublin for Anjelica Huston's movie *The Mammy*, Tom repeatedly fluffed his two lines. He was required to deliver a brief dedication to Anjelica's character before launching into 'She's A Lady', but couldn't get it right. His eventual explanation proved that his healthy sense of humour was alive and well. 'It's these teeth,' he chuckled. 'They keep falling out.'

Tom and Annette Be
the world in Mars A

'Knickers. And, er... knickers.
Knickers everywhere.'

CHAPTER NINE

KNICKERS

Fads may come and fashions may go, but knickers remain for ever. In Tom Jones's career they've become something of a millstone around his ankles. No matter how often he says he's older and more dignified now, and would prefer his audiences to pay attention to the music, the knickers just will not be dropped.

Even in 1999, comedian Eddie Izzard introduced the singer on-stage at the Royal Albert Hall, at a concert in memory of the late Linda McCartney, by mumbling, 'Knickers. And, er... knickers. Knickers everywhere.' It's understandable if, after all these years, Tom is tired of being tired of this hardy perennial joke of a routine. Although he's said his devoted, loyal fans are 'absolutely terrific', it's no secret that he was particularly gratified by the attention of a younger generation after his eighties chart comeback with 'Kiss', and that his management sought to nurture this appeal. They attempted to phase out 'the knickers thing', but it just wouldn't go away.

It began, according to Tom, in New York in 1968, at the Copacabana, and grew in popularity in Vegas. In '66, speaking to the *Daily Mirror*, a bejewelled Tom had told Donald Zec, 'I'm trying to get across that I'm alive when I sing. All of it – the emotion, the sex, the power, the heartbeat and the bloodstream. And the words don't mean as much unless the body gets into the act. Al Jolson got on his knees! Danny Kaye makes with the hips. All the best coloured singers move, man, move! I admit I shove it a bit but I don't spell it out like P. J. Proby.'

So why, he was asked, were you labelled obscene on tour in Australia?

'Because I took my shirt off during the show.'

Why?

'Because it was bloody hot. In Brisbane a copper came into the dressing room, poked me in the chest and warned me. I felt like butting him with the nut but my hair had just been combed for the act.'

Tom's act has always encouraged frenzy from the fans.

'It's the closest thing to sex that I do,' he told Chrissy Iley of the *Daily Mail* in '89. 'The adoration from the fans is very sexual. My ego needs it; I thrive on it. My biggest fear is that someone will stop me. I have dreams where I'm locked up and have to murder someone to get free. Anything to not be locked up...

'I got mobbed the other day... I can't believe they're doing it for an old-timer like me!'

'After my stage show I just dive in the shower and feel like I've performed some great sexual act. I don't think I'd've got where I am today without being so attractive to women.

'I like to think I'm a normal, healthy, red-blooded man who doesn't take drugs and who isn't bent,' he said in '83. 'What I do on stage is exactly the way I feel. It's not a false image.'

As time went on, he saw the funny side of things. By the late eighties he was chortling to the *Sun*, 'I got mobbed the other day... I thought that was reserved for Duran Duran and George Michael – I can't believe they're doing it for an old-timer like me! The fantastic thing is that the last time I was on *Top of the Pops* they thought I was the outrageous one, with my tight trousers and my shirt unbuttoned. That was considered suggestive. Now I'm the traditional one!'

So much so, that when a girl in Liverpool asked him to sign her bare breasts, Tom told her to cover herself up, agreeing under pressure only to sign her back. 'As for the knickers and keys on-stage, I just hold them up to the band and yell, "Party tonight, lads!", then throw them back. The other night one girl shouted, "Tom Jones, I want your child!" So I grabbed Mark, my thirty-something son and manager, and said, "Here he is! Take him!"'

In '87, Tom explained to the *Daily Mail*'s Lynda Lee-Potter that if his tie and jacket were liable to come off during his performance, 'It's like foreplay in sex rather than just jumping on somebody. I've learnt what works by trial and error. The women get excited. I perspire a lot, and I used to be a bit self-conscious about it, but women handed me their hankies to wipe my brow and then wanted them back – so that's become part of the act. Wearing tight trousers rather than loose ones... well, that just seems to work.'

It was son Mark's wife, Donna, who tried to wind down the knicker-hurling phenomenon – possibly a misguided PR debacle on a par with Coca-Cola's stab, mid-eighties, at changing its classic formula. An obedient 57-year-old Tom commented on her idea of nixing the barrage of lingerie: 'The underwear has always been the focus in reviews, so Donna said we should get the point across that we don't want it to happen any more.' Yet Tom couldn't restrain his instincts. 'But I told her you can't stop something that's been happening for thirty years. I don't think I want to stop it anyway. If you're singing sexy songs to get a sexy reaction, then this is it. As long as it doesn't interfere with the show.'

At early shows Tom had mopped his brow with undies. 'I used to use them as props and think it was all a bit of fun. Then I realised it was all getting a bit tacky.' He now made a promise. 'The women will still throw them, but I won't pick them up any more.'

A difficult vow to fulfil. A Comic Relief sketch saw Tom and Lenny Henry competing as to who was the premier Mr Sexy. Henry could not oust the master. Comic Relief gave Tom the chance to show that he didn't really believe in the Medallion man thing. Similarly, Jonathan Ross's *Last Resort* show saw Tom pelted with a plethora of panties.

So intrigued were the British media by the 'bricklayer in a blouse's new standards of decency that journalist Martyn Harris inquired if Tom had checked the 'blizzard of underwear' for 'hygiene'.

'Oh,' replied Tom, deadpan, 'I have a good look at the knickers, you know. But the British women's ones are always laundered and ironed in their handbags.' Only if a fan was very persistent would Tom accept their drawers. 'It's difficult then; you don't want to seem ungrateful.'

In truth, the ritual shouldn't have been taken so earnestly. It was comic relief on a giant, if tawdry, scale. The knickers had now become symbolic rather than coded, waved aloft like football banners. Parodic, ocean-sized bloomers with lofty waistbands and elasticated legs were not uncommon. In a typically British manner, the initially erotic had become the seaside-postcard, *Carry On*-style, farcical.

'"Hey, Tom, you pump up the tyres, but it's me that gets to ride the bike."'

An easy-going Tom told Harris, 'I'm not as pure as the driven snow, but I'm not as naughty as the papers say. A husband came up to me after a show once and said, "Hey, Tom, you pump up the tyres, but it's me that gets to ride the bike."'

Tom, while still kicking up a rumpus on-stage, was settling more comfortably into middle age than a reputed Lothario is generally supposed to. 'A lot of young women come to my shows,' he told the *Daily Express* in '91, on the verge of a 25-date British tour, 'and find me just as sexy as the older ones do. But I do think they're looking at me as a fifty-year-old man. You can look at somebody older and think they're sexy without wanting to go to bed with them. Whereas, when I was younger, a lot of my fans were my age and were definitely wanting to go to bed with me. Now, although it's a sexy act, I don't take myself seriously as a sex object.'

Although he's said that if a girl got up on stage and wanted to kiss him he wouldn't complain, that would be as far as it went. 'I was never tempted to leave my wife. We may have homes in two countries but we're always in one of them together, when I'm not touring. I'd be lying if I said my head wasn't ever turned by some great-looking bird, but then someone might be nineteen and beautiful on the outside, but so what? What is she on the inside?

'Youth,' continued Tom, nodding sagely, 'isn't everything.' However he added, as an afterthought, 'When we married, my wife was sixteen and I was seventeen and we were inseparable. They were the best times.'

'The other night one girl shouted,
"Tom Jones, I want your child!"
So I grabbed Mark, my thirty-something son
and manager, and said,
"Here he is! Take him!"'

'The knicker-throwing has decreased over the years, but it's still there. And they still yell, "Get 'em off."'

Whatever ardent pleas incoming management teams may have made to the contrary, knickers and Tom Jones maintain their seriocomic, semiotic, symbiotic relationship. 'The knicker-throwing has decreased over the years, but it's still there. And they still yell, "Get 'em off." What irritates me is when a concert is reviewed and it's: "This artist sang that number and that artist sang this number and... underwear was thrown at Tom Jones."

'You could say that I want more credibility now,' he told the *Express* in '92. 'I've always wanted to make good music and it began to hurt my pride that they weren't listening, they were just waiting to throw their knickers at me. I don't feel fifty-two: only when I look in the mirror does it remind me that I'm no longer thirty. But I'm not saying I'm fed up with people thinking I'm sexy. I just don't want my image to be tatty or cheap. I might get to an age where I'll look silly. I don't want to become a caricature of myself. I'm not saying give in to your age; just that I want to do my best and do it gracefully. I could afford to do nothing, but that'd be boring. I want to compete – I know I still have a great voice. It's still there, so why not?

'Only the public can decide how big you are,' he'd reflected on an earlier occasion. 'I don't need to charm anyone in the business, because I don't need anyone to owe me anything. But if the public stopped coming to see me, then I'd be in trouble. The only time I feel comfortable and in control of the situation is when I'm playing to a full house.'

There existed a dilemma, however, which the singer recognised. 'I don't mind taking the p*ss out of myself,' he told another interviewer.

Thus one Paula Yates, writing in the *Sunday Mirror* magazine in '93, was able to elicit the statement, 'I didn't wipe my nose on them, just my forehead! It's just fun and games; it shouldn't get in the way of the music.' She observed that Tom was sweating so much, she wondered 'if I should slip out of my large navy knickers and hand them to him to wipe his brow. I decide that it might make him feel worse.'

American actress Brooke Shields, at the time married to tennis ace Andre Agassi, went one better. On US television she confessed, 'When Tom started swivelling his hips and doing that whole "Delilah" thing I had to scream. I ran up on-stage and started dancing with him, but because of the lighting the security people couldn't see who I was and tried to get me down.

'Maybe I shouldn't have reacted by getting carried away and waving my knickers in the air. I knew that was a bad idea.'

'I was not just close to Gordon.
He was as near to me as a brother, my dear,
dear friend, my adviser... a part of my life.'

CHAPTER TEN

THE SON ALSO RISES

Tuesday 5 August 1986 was one of the saddest days of Tom Jones's life. He helped carry Gordon Mills's coffin to a grave under the trees in a Surrey cemetery. Wearing black glasses, with his chin stuck firmly into his broad chest, he said goodbye to the man who made him a star. 'I was not just close to Gordon,' he said. 'He was as near to me as a brother, my dear, dear friend, my adviser... a part of my life. He took care of my life, and now I'll have to learn to deal with it...'

A still-jetlagged Jones had flown from New York by Concorde, then travelled in a Rolls-Royce to Hersham for the funeral. It was the first time he'd visited Britain in three years.

He and Mills had climbed from the Rhondda valleys to the pinnacle of the showbiz mountain together. Once there, they'd shared a luxurious lifestyle and palatial homes – a striking contrast to the terraces they'd grown up in.

'When Gordon came to Wales and we met, he said that I should be up in London making records,' Tom told the *Daily Mail*'s John Edwards that day. 'Now it wasn't the first time I'd heard that, but the difference was that Gordon actually did something about it.

'He taught me just about everything. He groomed me, taught me my pacing. He tried to be me sitting in the audience watching myself, and then told me how I'd criticise myself. He said he'd guide me to become larger than life. There are parts of me which he created totally. We were much more than brothers. As we were both very Welsh, we could get very vocal with each other at times, but we'd always get it straightened out.'

Only a month before, it transpired, Tom and the 51-year-old Gordon had been in an LA recording studio, when Gordon complained of stomach pains. The subsequent hospital tests showed these to be symptoms of cancer. Gordon's condition quickly deteriorated. On his final visit to Cedars Sinai hospital, Tom realised what was happening. 'He didn't look his normal self. He was no longer there; there was no hope. I just wanted to pick him up and take him home. He was dying in front of me.

'Gordon was a gambler, and thought odds of fifty-fifty, which I'd optimistically told him were the chances when he asked me, were reasonable. "That's not bad," he said. He was dead the next day; gone.'

Tom couldn't speak to the newspaper any more. A friend said intensely, 'Gordon lived fast. He was supposed to go out in a car crash at 200 mph, not from cancer.'

The obituaries hailed Mills as a 'kingmaker', noting that he went from being a bus conductor to one of the most powerful men in the entertainment industry. That he'd been a conservationist who at one time owned the world's largest private collection of orang-utans. They mentioned his film-star looks, his charisma, that a brief period in the army, which he hated, had taught him 'self-discipline, personal hygiene and self-respect'. They reported also that when Mills's friend Gerry Dorsey asked for 'the Tom Jones treatment', Mills rechristened him Engelbert Humperdinck ('in the borrowed robes of the composer of *Hansel and Gretel*') and ushered 'Release Me' his way, and that he'd transformed a 'kid in a funny cap', Raymond O'Sullivan, into 'Alone Again, Naturally' singer/songwriter Gilbert O'Sullivan (whose number one 'Clare' was inspired by Mills's small daughter – before, obviously, O'Sullivan's court action against Mills).

Three years later, when an obtuse interviewer asked if his macho image concealed a fear of facing up to vulnerability and suffering, Tom Jones replied, 'No no no... I've been upset and faced it. When my father died. And when my manager Gordon Mills died. He was like a blood brother. As he co-wrote "It's Not Unusual", it nearly chokes me to perform it even this long afterwards.'

It was time for his son, Mark Woodward, to step out of the wings and seize control. Described previously as a shy, awkward observer, he'd had plenty of time, and on-the-road experience, to work out what he'd change and why. Some members of the inner circle have said that Mark never really liked Gordon, despite the older man's efforts to teach

him the ways of management. There may have been some jealousy involved.
Ruthless changes and cutbacks initiated by Mark and his wife Donna after the transition
didn't help relationships between the two camps, or families.

Whatever Mark's reputation as a meek individual, he brought about a watershed
period in his father's career. After eighteen years of Vegas and similar schmaltz, Tom had
been a long time without a British hit. His record contract had been treading water for
years with the country wing of the Polygram label in America. Tom needed to break loose
from this sterile, six-album deal, and rediscover his roots, and Mark, at 29 an avid pop
and new wave fan, knew it.

Mark first supervised a revamp of his dad's image. The lace, frills, flares and hair
were trimmed. The eighties 'futuristic leatherette' look – in retrospect risible, but at the
time all the rage from Billy Idol to Wham! – came in. Tom, not for the first time,
underwent plastic surgery in an attempt to stay youthful, having bags removed from around
his eyes. Some of the older musicians in his band were clinically fired. Mark played Tom
new records; songs by such artists as INXS ('I Need You Tonight') and Prince emerged
in his shows. Prince's 'Kiss', in particular, with its funky rhythms and nudge-nudge lyrics,
seemed perfect for Tom. In fact, it was about to give the singer a new lease of life.

First, though, he had to reintroduce himself to the charts, and to Britain. This he did
with the in-some-ways aptly named 'The Boy From Nowhere'. Out of the blue, Tom Jones
was back.

'The Boy From Nowhere', a big ballad, was hardly the new-style, fashionable
Tom Jones we were about to meet. But it put his voice back in the charts in '87, and eased
the lock for his long-time, loyal fans. Taken from the musical *Matador*, based on the life
of sixties bullfighter El Cordobes, it told of 'a rags-to-riches story that could have been

Tom with son Mark displaying

some of the symbols of their suc

his own, says this rough-hewn man', wrote *Melody Maker*. Tom was at the time tipped to play the lead role in the musical when it opened in the West End the following summer. It was ultimately shelved when the real-life El Cordobes objected.

His first ample hit in fourteen years, it prompted Tom to tell the *Sun*, 'It's bloody amazing. I can't remember the last time I got such a reaction – and from young kids too! I'm even getting requests for interviews from trendy music papers. And I'm told that all the Northern Soul clubs are playing 'It's Not Unusual' again, and that's twenty-two years old!

'I don't spend my whole life in a tuxedo, you know. I wear denims, too. I still know what young audiences want.'

'I don't spend my whole life in a tuxedo, you know. I wear denims, too. I still know what young audiences want.'

He certainly knew what Jonathan Ross wanted. The call from the TV presenter's show *The Last Resort* came soon afterwards. 'They said this is not a plug show,' Jones told the *Guardian*. 'Jonathan Ross said, "We'd rather you didn't do 'The Boy From Nowhere' and did something else, something... up."' Tom named a few songs he was doing in his live set, including 'Kiss'. 'He said, "What – the Prince one? Do you fancy giving that a go?" I said, "We'll do that then."'

Tom's ultra-confident, show-stopping performance tore the screen apart and was talked about for days. 'It's weird,' said Tom, 'I'm always doing stuff like that in my stage show, but if people don't come to see it they don't know. And as I haven't recorded anything like that for years, they're saying, "We didn't know Tom Jones did that kind of thing."'

'Success is the best revenge,' Tom laughed, as 'Kiss' roared into the Top Ten, assisted by a nifty video which voguishly dressed Tom in an over-large, David Byrne-style, 'post-modern, ironic' suit. Free from the country contract which tied him to cultish American-only releases 'I wanted to make modern records' he was asked to sign to Jive Records, 'to make a hot, contemporary album.'

Two members of the then-hip, avant-garde instrumental combo The Art Of Noise, Anne Dudley and J.J. Jeczalik, saw the 'Kiss' rendition on TV. They'd recently reinvented

'We've always been close,' Tom asserted. 'He's been on the road with me since he was seventeen and we're very alike.' The father and son combination shared a love of a drink or two. Or eight. When papers asked if it was true that he and Mark, as recounted by Jonathan Ross, had sunk eight pints each in a quick session between flights at an airport, Tom laughed, 'Oh, it was more than that, I hope!'

The *News of the World*, buying the story of former minder Chris Montgomery in '91, took a sceptical view of their working rapport. They reported that Mark often ordered Tom to remove his chunky gold rings before a show, and that Tom was submissive and obedient. 'Off-stage the singer who makes women want to surrender is under the thumb,' Montgomery sneered. It was said that Tom knew his macho image couldn't go on for ever, and that if he was to 'do a Sinatra' and carry on performing into old age, 'he knows he must knuckle down to the gentle bullying of his manager son Mark and wife Linda.'

Mark thought fans should concentrate on Tom's singing, not his trousers.

Mark thought fans should concentrate on Tom's singing, not his trousers. He was 'trying to refocus their attention three feet up from where they used to look. He's also tried to get his dad to tone down the famous hip-grinding and pelvic thrusts that drive audiences wild.'

Tom, it was said, submitted without a word of protest, even during 'stomach in, chest out' photo sessions. 'Mark's the boss. Whatever he says goes. There's been a complete reversal of roles. Tom does nothing without permission or approval from his son.'

It seemed Mark had indeed learnt a thing or two from Gordon Mills, and was adapting his standards to more forward-looking sounds and styles. Tom had recently undergone a scalp operation to hide a bald patch, and was a frequent babysitter for Mark and wife Donna. He was even said to be cutting down on his girl-chasing, after Mark was annoyed about the embarrassment caused by the Katherine Berkery paternity suit. But there's only so far a showbiz legend can go in that direction. 'I've had to smuggle girls out of the back of the house so Mark wouldn't see them and give his dad a hard time,' said Montgomery.

Yet it seemed the two still got on like a house on fire. Even Montgomery was forced to concede, 'I've seen them get through a thousand pounds' worth of champagne in one sitting at a bar.'

'Fads may come and go but true quality never wanes... The man is the best rock 'n' roll voice Britain ever produced.'

CHAPTER ELEVEN

THE 90s, AND HOW TO SWING IN THEM

Tom Jones swaggered out of the eighties into the nineties with new credibility, a new direction and, whether he liked it or not, an undiminished weight of lingerie nestling on-stage at his feet. His reputation had been reassessed after the comeback of 'Kiss' (also a hit in America), and the fallow country period left behind. He'd always enjoyed duets and collaborations with other singers, and was to experiment in this mode throughout the decade. Critics approached him, if not entirely seriously, at least with a half-ironic, half-genuine respect bordering on 'we are not worthy' awe.

Melody Maker's Kris Kirk sighed, 'Fads may come and go but true quality never wanes... The man is the best rock 'n' roll voice Britain ever produced, Billy Fury included.' In the *NME*, Kevin Davies wrote, 'The man is built like a brick sh*thouse... concealed inside that frame is one of the most powerful voices known to nature, The Jones Voice,' while *Guardian* reviewer Caroline Sullivan gushed of Tom's 1989 Hammersmith Odeon show: 'Tom Jones is a risible Las Vegas hack with no relevance to contemporary music? Wrong! If you have ever thrilled to pop music, you would have been Watusiing in the aisles during this gig. He doesn't so much dance as occasionally stop short to briefly rotate his pelvis in the lewdest manner possible. And there are more than a few hungry-eyed teenage lovelettes in the front rows, all speculating on the source of the outlandish convexity at the front of his black 501s... I found myself at the foot of the stage, brandishing a hankie, with about fifteen other women...'

'I know I'm not ugly, but I'm not handsome either. But I think I must be attractive – when people tell you that all the time, it rubs off on you.'

Tom was aware of the shift in public perception, and milked it, more than happy with his new manager. 'I'm hip again,' he observed correctly. 'There's a buzz about me again.' He added thoughtfully, 'I know I'm not ugly, but I'm not handsome either. But I think I must be attractive – when people tell you that all the time, it rubs off on you.'

In the *People*, in a '91 feature, Mary Kemp cooed, 'His eyes just follow every movement you make, taking in the way you smooth your skirt or drink your coffee. He certainly makes you feel good, as if you're the most beautiful girl in the world.'

He wasn't slow to generously praise contemporary artists either. George Michael was 'a great songwriter and an excellent live singer,' he opined, 'with plenty of staying power.' Madonna? 'A girl who's got everything. She can sing, dance, and hold a crowd in her hand.' As for Boy George, 'Now he's stopped wearing all his crazy clothes you can see the talent clearly.'

On the other hand, Tom was quoted in 1990 discussing his singing peers in rather less flattering terms. Mick Jagger, he was alleged to have said, 'knows he doesn't have a good voice so he does the best with the tools he has.' Cliff Richard was 'mild... like going through life on tranquillisers.' As for Phil Collins, he 'makes a monotonous piercing sound with no sex or warmth.' 'I don't understand how they do so well,' he went on, 'or what people think they're listening to – especially the women.'

Tom's album of that year betrayed an uncertainty as to whether to flirt with the new or go steady with the old. An unlikely collaboration with Van Morrison, 'Carrying A Torch', mystified more people than it moved. 'It was definitely Van Morrison music, which is fine, but after doing "Kiss" I'd wanted to do more of that,' Tom told Adam Sweeting in '94 in the *Guardian*. 'Even when I was recording with Van, the black organist had said, "When are you going to do another 'Kiss'?" I realised that song had hit a nerve. So this album didn't really work. It's like it never really existed... which is fine. As far as people are concerned, "Kiss" was the last record.

'Memories are great, but you've got to go with the flow. Move on; don't get stuck in old sounds.'

Fellow Celt Morrison, legendarily grumpy, had written and produced half the album, and the title track had apologetically nudged the bottom end of the singles chart. On its release, Tom had been more positive, telling *The Times*, 'I've always had that problem of finding the right material, especially nowadays. Most writers are performers and do the songs themselves, so it's hard to get first crack at it. For me, it's like the difference between actors and scriptwriters. I find it easy to put over a good song, but I can't write. Van came over with these songs for me to listen to and I thought, How the hell do you come up with these things?'

'Memories are great, but you've got to go with the flow. Move on; don't get stuck in old sounds.'

Unfortunately, the album neither sold well or capitalised on Tom's blossoming 'retro-cool' image. His light-hearted TV appearances, however, kept him in the public eye and displayed his revived sense of humour. First with Jonathan Ross, then with Lenny Henry as Theophilus P. Wildebeest for Comic Relief, he showed his comic chops, sending up his sex-god image. For the latter he willingly sported a huge codpiece, from the groin of which there burst forth a flashing red nose. 'I've always said I don't take myself seriously,' Tom reiterated.

By '92, he was 'appearing' on an altogether hipper comedy show – Matt Groening's American slice of animated genius *The Simpsons*. 'Tom's was more than a walk-on part – the whole episode centred on Marge Simpson's liking for the 'guest star'. Working at a nuclear power plant alongside hapless husband Homer, she suggested the company boost morale by piping in Tom Jones music. 'That always cheers me up!' announced Marge, beaming. 'What's New Pussycat?' blazed across the airwaves of Springfield. All ended well after a customarily surreal plot involving the kidnapping of a 'cartoon' Tom, Marge's heart fluttering, and dastardly deeds by Mr Burns. Tom's alter ego was chained to a radiator by Burns, who offered Marge her idol as a gift in a vain attempt to seduce her. The show's executive producer said all the writers were fans, especially the women.

The same year found Tom meeting his wanton, licentious match on another American TV special, *Sandra After Dark*. This was a vehicle for Sandra Bernhard, the left-field singer-actress-comedienne, who after catching Tom's act in Vegas (a zipcode and cash-cow which Tom wasn't neglecting despite his renascent British profile), begged him to duet with her. 'He's such a pro,' she squealed, 'and never lost his sex appeal.'

Tom with his grandchildren,
Alexander and Emma.

The series gamely attempted to trace the roots and evolution of pop music, and Tom was a genuinely interested, and indeed prestigious, host. It was shown on Channel 4 in the UK and also sold to America. Fortunately, Tom's original idea for a name for the series – *Keep Your Knickers On* – was outvoted. As his first major British TV production since the seventies, it was an important project.

Tom told the *Daily Telegraph* it would 'explain where pop music came from.' Guest stars agreed to cover their favourite songs and chat with Tom about their influences. 'It's not a chat show or a live music show; it's somewhere in between – a kind of seminar-cum-workshop of pop,' wrote Jasper Rees. On the opening show, EMF's 'Unbelievable' 'lined up alongside Erasure, playing Abba's 'S.O.S.', Marianne Faithfull singing 'The Ballad Of Lucy Jordan' and Shakespear's Sister attempting T. Rex's 'Hot Love'. Meanwhile, Tom topped the lot with versions of The Beatles' 'Come Together' and Bruce Springsteen's 'Dancing In The Dark'. For future shows he promised appearances by Joe Cocker, The Chieftains, Pops Staples, Cyndi Lauper, Mica Paris and Curtis Stigers, among others. Jones was adamant that he's been dodging pigeon-holes for three decades and couldn't be better suited to the format.

'I'm not in one area of music, and never have been. Central TV said I could do whatever I liked... I want to see something in print about my voice for a change. It'll cover the development of pop music from turn of the century to present-day funk, metal and rap – and it's gonna be fun.'

The day after the first show, the *Evening Standard's* Mark Steyn adopted a sarcastic stance when reviewing Tom' rendition of 'I've Got You Under My Skin'. 'I don't know what he's got under his skin,' he wrote, 'but all those strange mouth movements suggest he's trying to dislodge a cornflake from his back teeth. On the other hand, you have to admire a series that starts with Cole Porter... then goes on to Hoagy Carmichael...'

Steyn was less generous to Tom's guests. 'Sadly, not all the guests shared Tom's broad historical perspective. Asked about their major influences, EMF cited dance music: "From Prince even to a lot of old stuff. I remember listening to Hot Chocolate," said one, as if he'd just remembered the name of Monteverdi's backing group... The interviews were the weakest link – in this respect, Tom's interviewing technique seems to be based on TVAM's Lorraine Kelly...' Steyn savaged Siobhan Fahey of Shakespear's Sister and Andy Bell of Erasure, before conceding, 'If Tom seems uncomfortable in the chit-chat, he's terrific in the songs... *The Right Time* throws the guests and Tom together and comes up with some surprisingly effective combinations. It's the closest TV's got to capturing the fun of live pop performance in quite a while, and it works mainly because Tom's at home with just about any song.'

Confirmed Tom: 'It's a chance to do the stuff I've always wanted to do – gospel, blues, soul and Celtic. I've been seen as a narrow balladeer, but what I like are performers with big, strong, straightforward songs, sometimes right over the top – just like me!'

The revival continued apace, Tom stealing the show at a benefit concert for the Brazilian rainforests at New York's Carnegie Hall. He nominally shared the bill with the likes of Sting, Bryan Adams, Tina Turner and George Michael, but famed R&B journalist Gerri Hirshey, author of *Nowhere to Run*, claimed, 'Only the majestic Tina Turner matched him for lung power and locomotion.' The American press, from the trad broadsheets to the cutting-edge style bibles, were in agreement. 'He's Mister Retro-Cool,'said *Entertainment Weekly*. 'Once again, Tom Jones is hot!'

'I find it easy to go on stage and do a two-hour show; it's no more difficult than it was thirty years ago.'

The BBC arts programme *Omnibus* clearly assented, having devoted a special Good Friday 1991 programme to him. 'I find it easy to go on-stage and do a two-hour show; it's no more difficult than it was thirty years ago,' he revealed. 'The only problem I find now is if I have to do two shows in one night.' So you can't do it twice a night any more, Tom? asked interviewer Sandra Parsons. 'Well, now, no, I didn't say that...' chuckled Tom.

'Singing is my hobby,' he added. 'Most people look forward to retiring so they can devote time to their hobby. But I'll keep on doing this till I can't... I dread that day. I'm glad to be here – Elvis was only forty-two when he died. The kick is still there; it's a tremendous feeling.'

In the same feature, Tom poignantly remembered playing on the same bill as The Rolling Stones many years back, and realising, as he bumped and ground through the songs, that many of the girls were actually frightened of him. 'I couldn't understand it, you know,' he says, in his soft, gravelly lilt. 'I wasn't doing anything different from Mick Jagger. Except he camped it up a bit more. Maybe I seemed a bit more real, and that scared them...'

Tom Jones: scarier than Jagger!

He also drew a typically frank comment from notorious American 'shock jock' Howard Stern, who announced live on air, 'I think the reason women used to throw their panties at you was because you have a big package in your pants. It's for real. It's not like you stuffed socks in there.'

'No,' replied Tom. 'No, I never did that.' Under pressure from Stern, he admitted that occasionally after a show he'd invite young models into his hotel room 'for a drink'.

'You're a Welshman,' said Stern sagely. 'And Welshmen are horny.'

Striking while the Welshman was hot in '93, Tom signed a new record deal with a more fashionable, hard-edged label. Interscope boasted among its roster such trendy left-field names as Snoop Doggy Dogg, Dr Dre and Nine Inch Nails, and was partly run by John McClain, who's masterminded Janet Jackson's career. The really surprising thing was that Tom Jones then made an album that was perhaps more ambitious and experimental than any of these acts.

Tom's deconstruction and reconstruction were complete. The album sold 40,000 copies in its first fortnight.

The magnificently named *The Lead and How To Swing It,* released in '94, saw Tom collaborating with such top-of-the-range producers as Flood (U2, Nine Inch Nails), Teddy Riley (swingbeat guru, Michael Jackson) and Youth (The Orb, Killing Joke), and writers and artists as cultish as The Wolfgang Press, Tori Amos (with whom he duetted) and DJ Battlecat. 'Whether he revels in the irony or is oblivious to it isn't entirely clear,' reckoned the *Guardian*'s Adam Sweeting. 'Although a man prepared to dress in a string vest and Sta-Prest trousers on the front of his album sleeve, and a red PVC suit on the back, is either doing it for a bet or has a great sense of humour.'

It seems the musicians involved took the affair rather more seriously. 'His power and passion and delivery remain unchallenged in contemporary pop music,' said Youth. The Wolfgang Press, the British indie group who penned the striking, minor hit 'If I Only Knew', raved, 'What Tom has that others today do not is soul and sex.'

Adam Sweeting remained suspicious. 'Who can say whether the joke's on us, for taking Jones's bizarre stylistic gyrations seriously, or on him, for deluding himself

that a fifty-four-year-old veteran of Vegas and the cabaret circuit could possibly be
a contender in the era of ambient dub and the Internet?'

Nevertheless, Tom's deconstruction and reconstruction were complete. The album
sold 40,000 copies in its first fortnight. He still sold out Vegas or Wembley Arena whenever
he played there, still split his time between the UK and the US, and still wowed crowds
young and old.

At '94's MTV Music Awards in Berlin, he held his own next to Take That,
Bjork and George Michael. 'It is the opinion of MTV,' said a spokeswoman, 'that Tom
Jones is COOL.' DJ John Peel chipped in with, 'I'd never have believed I'd be jumping up
and down shouting for "Delilah", but when I saw Tom Jones perform he was wonderful.'
Rolling Stone magazine nominated his LA gig at House Of Blues as best live show of
the year: 'We screamed like a couple of tipsy housewives on an annual girls' night out...
I guess that's the magic of Tom Jones.'

Despite having shared stages with the likes of Elvis and Sammy Davis Jr, Tom was
still keen to keep in touch with young tastes. He wasn't averse to duetting with New Model
Army, or discussing plans for a musical with Malcolm McLaren. Perhaps the zenith of
this comeback occurred when Tom won over an initially suspicious throng at the 1995
Glastonbury Festival. He recalls seeing thousands of scruffy indie kids rushing over the hill
towards the stage as he began. Specifically, he remembered watching a huge banner on poles
being unfurled. It read: 'Tom F*cking Jones!' 'That's me,' he chortled. 'That's me all
right – Tom F*cking Jones! Wouldn't it be great to use that all the time?'

With rockers New Model Army

for a video shoot.

*'I'm going to do a duet with the mighty
Tom Jones, he's my hero!'*

CHAPTER TWELVE

WHAT'S NEW PUSSYCAT?

By 1998 Tom was fully established as a living, breathing icon of the art of strut.
Whether his stuff was received ironically or innocently mattered little to him. He hit on
another masterstroke at that year's music industry Brit Awards in February.

It was announced by a panting, breathless press that Tom and swaggerer-du-jour,
former Take That imp Robbie Williams, were to perform a duet – a medley of songs from
the recent record-breaking British movie *The Full Monty*. Fittingly, this was a film about
working-class strippers.

Their seven-minute slot was to include what the *Sun* referred to as 'Tom's raunchy
classic', 'You Can Leave Your Hat On', as well as Steve Harley and Cockney Rebel's
'Make Me Smile' and the Wilson Pickett evergreen, 'Land Of 1,000 Dances' – a number
Tom had probably sung at least a thousand times before. Still, it was an exciting moment
for young Robbie. 'I'm going to do a duet with the mighty Tom Jones,' he beamed.
'He's my hero!'

A Brits spokesman rather shattered the illusion by mumbling, 'The producers were
disappointed they couldn't get Radiohead or Prodigy to play, but this more than makes up

Tom duets with Robbie Williams

at the Brit Awards, 1998.

for it. It's the icing on the cake – two generations coming together on songs from a great British film.'

The show went well, although as one broadsheet noted, Tom was the cooler of the duo. 'Robbie Williams performed what can only be described as an act of worship...'

'He was a bit flirtatious,' admitted Tom. 'I think he's great – I get off on the respect of young performers.'

Tom Jones: too sexy for television! Too dangerous for Essex!

Not everybody got off on the show in quite the same even-tempered way. One Mitch Charles from Ilford complained to the *Sun* the next day, after his television set had exploded while Tom 'jiggled his hips'.

'It definitely was unusual,' said the Essex man. 'The TV has been fine for six years, but it couldn't take the Welshman's movements. The second he jumped on-stage and gyrated his hips there was a big bang and smoke started pouring out of the back of it. The picture went dead and there was an awful smell.'

The sad BT worker went on to moan, 'I might have to bill Tom for a new TV. He' got millions, more than enough money to buy us a nice plush telly with a remote control. This one is only good for the knacker's yard... a bit like Tom, I suppose.'

Tom Jones: too sexy for television! Too dangerous for Essex!

Later that year, Tom was also to prove too rock 'n' roll for most of today's
squeaky-clean pop stars. He sang several numbers, including 'Delilah' and 'You Can Leave
Your Hat On', at the Prince's Trust Party In The Park. This charity show, organised by
Capital Radio, took place at Hyde Park in July, in front of around 100,000 spectators.
Also on the bill were Lionel Richie, All Saints, Natalie Imbruglia, The Corrs, B*Witched,
Boyzone, Gary Barlow, Shania Twain and Del Amitri, as well as compere Stephen Fry.

'He may be fifty-eight, he may have teenage grandchildren – but Tom Jones is
still the undisputed champion of the world,' claimed Victoria Coren's broadsheet review.
'He's the sultan of sex, the baron of ballads, the ruler of rock. When he took to the stage,
one can only hope that Prince Charles felt obliged to make a respectful bow.'

Apparently, at the backstage party afterwards, Tom wiped the floor with the young
pretenders. 'Oh, I was there till five in the morning as usual,' he said, shrugging.
Then added, on reflection, 'Could have been six.

'Of the other performers, only Boyzone were still at it. They're good lads – they enjoy
a drink.'

'My voice has more weight to it now… there's an edge to it that comes from just having lived longer.'

Such hedonism didn't hinder Tom's workaholic tendencies. He got some more film work in, with the aforementioned *Mars Attacks!* and Anjelica Huston's *The Mammy* ('playing myself again because her character is a big Tom Jones fan').

'If the parts are right, I'll do more. You can't turn the clock back, but I wonder what would've happened if I'd done more acting earlier. I'd love to have done a Western – all men are boys at heart, and you can't help fancying yourself on a horse with a gun on your hip.'

Hip he was, despite having to accept that he wasn't 25 any more. But there were benefits. 'My voice has more weight to it now… there's an edge to it that comes from just having lived longer. After you've been around a bit, you can put more into a lyric because you read more into it.'

While Tom tours for most of the year, his old records appear almost obligatorily on movie soundtracks both British and American, as ironic counterpoints and sincerely emotive heart-tuggers. His Christmas TV special of '96, *Tom Jones – For One Night Only*, saw him belting out oldies like 'Delilah' and 'It's Not Unusual', while duetting with artists ranging from soul diva Toni Braxton to former Dire Straits guitarist Mark Knopfler to operatic baritone and fellow Best Loved Welshman, Bryn Terfel. An institution, still standing but staunchly swinging.

One of the ultimate accolades came Tom's way in March 1998 when two rising bands of the era combined to propel a song composed in his honour into the top three. 'The Ballad Of Tom Jones' told the tale of a dysfunctional, fighting couple who resolve their differences after playing the golden hits of the Welshman once accused by the Duke of Edinburgh of 'gargling in gravel' (the Duke later apologised). 'I must be doing something right, then,' remarked Tom. The single, by Space, featured guest vocals by Cerys Matthews of Welsh band Catatonia, a true Tom fan. To gild the lily, the moniker of Space's Scouse singer was Tommy Scott. Now, where had Tom heard that name before?

On the domestic front, it appeared that Tom and Linda divided the year, with all four of their parents having now passed away, between homes in California and Wales. They bought a new house in the hills above LA, the house formerly belonging to Dean Martin and then Tom Jones now inhabited by movie star Nicolas Cage.

To all the ongoing tabloid allegations and scandals, as ever-present in Britain as the rain, an exasperated but resigned Tom has said, 'At least it's natural stuff. I mean… you know, nobody's suggesting that I had sex with kids or anything. Or sheep.'

Opposite: (Clockwise from top left) Mark Knopfler, Bryn Terfel, Tom and Toni Braxton.

'Tom has a remarkable ability to reinvent himself for each succeeding generation.'

RELOAD!

Tom's sung many times at Cardiff Arms Park, but in 1999 that annual emotional outpouring requiring his services and nobody else's (unless Shirley Bassey was in town) – the Wales versus England rugby match – took place at Twickenham. A storming 'Green, Green Grass Of Home' (of course), a full-blooded 'Delilah' and a faultless national anthem saw 40,000 Welshmen singing along with the maestro in brilliant sunshine. Inspirational stuff – underdogs Wales, much to Tom's delight, went on to snatch victory over the patronising enemy in the last seconds, for the first time in years.

The same mid-April weekend, Tom appeared at the Linda McCartney memorial concert at the Royal Albert Hall, as part of a bill including concert organiser Chrissie Hynde and her Pretenders, Elvis Costello, George Michael, Johnny Marr, Sinead O'Connor, Lynden David Hall, Neil Finn and, of course, Sir Paul McCartney. Tom Jones, OBE, rattled through The Beatles' 'She's A Woman' before bringing a tear to every eye with a version of 'Green, Green Grass Of Home' which featured a backing vocals trio of Chrissie Hynde, Sinead O'Connor and Des'ree, each of whom received a peck on the cheek from a gallant Mr Jones. 'Thank you, ladies,' he purred. Eddie Izzard, compering, got a big, unpretentious, blokish wink. Tom also sang 'Green, Green Grass Of Home' and joined in with a host of celebrities on a rousing chrous of 'Everyday When I Wake Up, I Thank The Lord I'm Welsh' at the concert given at Cardiff Castle to mark the opening of the Welsh Assembly.

Inset: Recording with Van Morrison.

Yet perhaps the most important landmark of Tom's 1999 will be the album of
duets - scheduled for release in September – he's currently beavering away at in the studio,
with a host of today's biggest rock names, from the indie-cred Welsh trio Stereophonics
to the grizzled Van Morrison. Robbie Williams is there, of course, as are Space and Cerys
Matthews' Catatonia. The Welsh flavour is further boosted by Manic Street Preachers'
involvement. Other starry names include All Saints, Natalie Imbruglia, The Cardigans,
Chrissie Hynde and Mick Hucknall, and there may be contributions from Heather Small,
The Divine Comedy, Barenaked Ladies and The James Taylor Quartet. The opus is being
produced by Stephen Hague, renowned for previous work with Robbie, the Manics,
New Order and The Pet Shop Boys. The 'executive producer' credits go to manager-son
Mark, and Gut Records (home of Space) chairman Guy Holmes, who's said, 'Tom has a
remarkable ability to reinvent himself for each succeeding generation. We know the esteem
in which he's held by stars who weren't even born when Tom made his first records.'

At the time of writing, it is rumoured that the results would include Tom
tackling INXS's 'Never Tear Us Apart' with Natalie Imbruglia, who's said, 'I thought
I'd be nervous – I kept thinking, My God, that's Tom Jones … and I'm singing with him!
I was so excited that I kept forgetting to do my bit!' Other tracks should include Three
Dog Night's 'Mama Told Me Not To Come' with Kelly from Stereophonics; Talking Heads'
'Burning Down The House' with The Cardigans; Elvis Presley's 'I'm Left, You're Right,

A backstage photocall with the
late Michael Hutchence of INXS.

She's Gone' with James from the Manics; 'Looking Out My Window' with The James Taylor Quartet; 'Sometimes We Cry', a new song with Van Morrison; 'Baby It's Cold Outside' with Cerys from Catatonia; Iggy Pop's 'Lust For Life' with Chrissie Hynde; Simply Red's Mick Hucknall on 'Ain't That A Lot Of Love'; Space on 'Little Did We Know'; Robbie Williams on Lenny Kravitz's 'Are You Gonna Go My Way'; and All Saints on the crowd-pleaser 'You Can Leave Your Hat On'.

Understandably, a television crew from Chris Evans' Ginger Productions has been filming at several of the recording sessions – a televised documentary is planned to coincide with the album release.

Welsh pop may now be resurgent, but for most of the entire life span of pop itself, one man has flown the flag.

'After the Brits appearance with Robbie Williams, kids kept coming up to me and asking who I was going to work with next,' said Tom. 'I thought, Let's go for it. It would have been boring just to bash out old stuff like "Delilah" – I'm flattered that these younger bands want to sing with me, and these are all songs that none of us has ever done before.

'I've had,' he continued, 'some of the best times singing with other singers and bands. I've always done it throughout my career. I'm very pleased these artists have said yes to the invitation, because I'm sure something very special is going to happen when we get down to working together.

'Every one of them is fresh and strong, no matter what kind of music they do, or how long they've been around. I'm absolutely thrilled to be having this experience.'

And so, no doubt, are they. Welsh pop may now be resurgent, but for most of the entire life span of pop itself, one man has flown the flag. From Pontypridd to Las Vegas, from *Top of the Pops* to the Harlem Apollo, the man whose voice and moves have raised the hemline of rock 'n' roll, soul, and ballads bigger than Babel, has always been larger than life and hungry-hearted. He'll celebrate his 60th birthday in June of the year 2000, and it's safe to say that, before they lay him beneath the green, green grass of home, the story of Tiger Tom The Twisting Vocalist has a few twists left in it yet.

BIBLIOGRAPHY

Books

Hildred, Stafford and Gritten, David, *Tom Jones: The Biography*, Sidgwick and Jackson, 1990, 1998

St Pierre, Roger, *Tom Jones – Quote Unquote*, Parragon, 1996

Newspapers

Daily Mail, 13 May 1989	116, 118
Daily Mail, 2 April 1987	86
Daily Mail, 20 April 1987	103
Daily Mail, 6 August 1986	125
Express, 21 March 1991	119
Express, 6 September 1983	98, 99
Guardian, 12 October 1998	129
Guardian, 2 June 1992	106, 122
Guardian, 22 November 1994	138
London Evening Standard, 6 June 1992	142
Mail On Sunday, 1 December 1998	147, 151
Mirror, 5 December 1966	53, 115
News Of The World, 12 March 1995	90
News Of The World, 17 December 1992	90
News Of The World, 20 October 1991	132
News Of The World, 23 December 1995	90
News Of The World, 9 January 1999	90
News of the World, 9 June 1974	85
Observer, 26 January 1969	93

People, 13 February 1983	116
People, 26 April 1992	102, 106
People, 4 September 1976	98, 111
Sun, 12 February 1998	150
Sun, 14 April 1987	116
Sun, 5 February 1998	149
Sunday Express, 19 April 1992	141
Sunday Express, 22 December 1996	140
Sunday Mirror, 6 June 1993	122
Daily Telegraph, 5 June 1992	142
The Times, 13 March 1991	131

Every attempt has been made to credit the source of quotations and any omissions are unintentional. Any such errors brought to the attention of Virgin Publishing will be corrected in a future edition.